Dave's Cunning Plans

The quest to mend broken Britain

By Ken Davidson

Contents

Preface

Dave's Cunning Plans tells the tale of the Con-Dem coalition and their plans to rebuild the broken landscape of Britain. The man with the blueprint is of course our leader, 'Call Me' Dave Cameron.

Dave has many plans, in fact, no area of your life will be left untouched by Dave's cunning, Dave has a plan for everything, well, perhaps not everything. Dave doesn't have much in the way of plan for elderly people or children in care, housing, transport or energy. And his plans for buzzards and badgers went south.

In fact, Dave's plans are not that cunning either, his plans may be callous and thoughtless like those for welfare reform, or deceitful like his plans for the NHS or slothful like those on lobbying and tax dodging, or dysfunctional like his relationship with Europe, or confused like his 'greenest government ever' campaign, or worse, they may be totally non-existent like his economic plans.

The purpose of this work is to provide a guide to what's been going on, for anyone who has successfully managed to sleep walk through the past four years, and I have to tell you, you've got a lot of catching up to do.

Introduction

Dave's Cunning Plans tells the tale of the 2010 Coalition Government, which nobody voted for, and its plans to reshape the landscape, to bring a new vision to this benighted land..... it's worse than Dave imagines.

When Baldrick announced to Black Adder, "I have a cunning plan", we knew that we would be treated in equal measure to an imaginative wheeze, coated with a thick layer of lunacy. Our current Prime Minister, Mr Cameron, henceforward, known simply as Dave, is no Baldrick but he does employ a large number of Baldricks. He actually keeps them under the stairs at No.10 Downing Street and consults them on a daily basis for his supply of cunning plans.

As you proceed you'll discover that much of what Dave is doing is just a continuation of New Labour's 'third way', i.e. a rag bag of borrowings from the wilting Empire of America, focused on dealing with the workshy. In truth Dave can be a bit reactive, not one of life's great thinkers, it's not easy being Dave but he does try to keep busy, continuing with the behaviour correction programmes of New Labour; privatising the space between your ears and the pores that allow your skin to breathe, all the bits that Mrs Thatcher didn't manage to get to.

When it comes to other matters, such as imperatives driven by global events, whether it's saving the planet from global warming, the Euro pantomime or Nato's 'humanitarian' interventions, Dave is just another cartoon character being boxed about the ears by some comedic sketch writer.

Dave is dealing with the deficit; largely by cutting the public sector and transferring its functions to private contractors, charities and communal good will. Dave's cutting to the bone because we simply can't afford the future!

Dave is driving out social decay; the detritus of welfare scrounging, benefit cheating, anti-social feckless festering underclass scum, and limbless incapacity claimants - he's contracted the best in the private sector for the clean up, although sometimes, they let him down.

In truth, Dave gets let down a lot, mainly by his colleagues; Liam Fox, Oliver Letwin, Chris Huhne, Andrew Mitchell, Jeremy Hunt, David Laws, Theresa May, Maria Miller, Francis Maude, Peter Cruddas, Andy Culson, Brooks Newmark, Douglas Carswell, Mark Reckless and Patrick Mercer have all let our leader down.

We're all in this together

At the Conservative Party Conference (Oct. 2010) Dave called on the country to "pull together" and said the Conservatives' slogan "We're all in this together" is "not a cry for help, but a call to arms". He finished by hailing the Tory Party as the party of national interest not vested interest, he repeated this again following the Queen's speech in May 2012 - for anyone who needed reminding.

At the time of Conference, twenty-two out of 29 cabinet ministers were millionaires, 19 out of 29 were educated at private, fee-paying schools and 19 out of 29 were Oxbridge graduates. We heard George Osborne announcing half a million job losses in the public sector, and did we hear his millionaire colleagues, in the spirit of togetherness, showing some empathy, no - we heard Iain Duncan Smith telling the jobless to get on their bikes, we heard Jeremy Hunt telling the poor to have fewer children, and Osborne himself accusing those on benefits of making it a "lifestyle choice".

The problem with the public school/Oxbridge contingent and their imitators is that life enables them to reach avenues that are closed to those who have chosen their parents less well and this sometimes leaves them a trifle out of touch with the common man. Sir Peter Viggers and his need for the public to provide his ducks with a nice little house (for £1,600) springs to mind, or perhaps, Douglas Hogg takes the top prize, he thought the common man should pay for his moat to be cleared out. In order to understand the beast we need to get inside the Tory mind, to understand the lexicon that these people live by.

That fortune smiles on those born on the right side of the tracks is unarguable and the manners and expectations they take on are a part of that inheritance, this lends itself to strong self-belief. The downside of being cursed thus is that when you are found wanting, you just can't believe that you're wrong. It's not just that your actions are being questioned, it's the inflexibility of your self-belief that damages your ability to deal with the challenges of the moment, this is a signal feature of Toryism.

Some would argue that making an issue of the wealth and privilege of Dave's political chums is just the politics of envy and they wouldn't be wrong. Half the world's capital is owned and controlled by less than 100 individuals, the political caste pay homage to these people and owe their privileged existence to the facilitation they provide for further accumulation. Those who talk of envy also believe that the wealth and privilege of the few is some kind of natural order, John Ball, the intellectual leader of the Peasants' Revolt, would have put them straight.

No matter, this is not an inquiry into why some people feel the need to spend their lives apologising for the behaviour of a bunch of carpet baggers. The thing is, you rarely hear a poor man proclaiming "We're all in this together" and you're hardly likely to, when the utterances of those who do, show utter contempt for low waged working people and those struggling on benefits. Leaving the feelings of the dispossessed to one side, hearing the Prime Minister tell us "We're all in this together" sounds very much like good old fashioned Tory patronage. Dave, himself, does like to keep in touch with the common man at Waitrose since he finds the customers there more "talkative and engaged" than the wider public. Altogether "a better class of shopper", he said. However, the Harvard Business School gave the phrase "We're all in this together" the thumbs up in a recent report (Aug, 2014) saying that workers performed 48% better when told their efforts were all about togetherness. (Note: the workers in question were American.)

Broken Britain

When Dave talks about Broken Britain he is being extremely cunning. His broken refrain is aimed at a particular target; the poor, the excluded, the dispossessed. All discussion, both from him and his top ministers, will be focussed on welfare cheats and freeloaders. Central to this discussion will be the lack of moral fibre among such types, their unwillingness to pull themselves up by their bootstraps. For such types the benefits system has encouraged an unwillingness to strive, it's the benefits system that's broken and Dave is going to fix it.

In sum, when Dave says Broken Britain, he doesn't mean the whole of Britain, he just means a few dark corners where the shameless dwell. However, you'll see as we scan across all Dave's policy agendas that pretty much everything is broken or was never whole in the first place.

Britain is one of the least equal among developed economies, this is not a natural feature of the landscape, it's a chronic design flaw. Economic inequality prevents genuine social progress, that is, a more caring and fairer society, a more enabling society and by extension, a more successful and innovative society. Britain's over-reliance on a few City high rollers, deckchair attendants and coffee vendors to put the jam on the bread has not served the nation well. Unfortunately, too many of the Baldricks that Dave surrounds himself with are of the opinion that inequality is the price you pay for a dynamic thrusting economy, where the competitive spirit, of necessity, will pulverize those too weak or unable to keep up - collateral damage.

Dave has a plan; his focus is on changing behaviour, re-adjusting expectations to fit with the reality of Broken Britain. Where the man from the Joseph Rowntree Foundation sees someone struggling to make ends meet, Dave sees the poverty of aspiration, not the poverty of resources. Dave's got his blueprint for Social Mobility to help out here, he's put Nick Clegg in charge of that one.

Dave thinks if only they would just read *Self Help* by Samuel Smiles, whilst forgetting he's closed all the libraries.... in fact, Dave can be a bit forgetful, he left his 9 year old daughter in the pub and went home to Chequers before he and Sam-Cam realised they'd left her behind. And witnessing his failure to "recollect" at the Leveson inquiry was just plain embarrassing.

On second thoughts, Leveson would have needed a lay down in a dark room if he had someone giving evidence who could remember anything. Leveson went on holiday after publishing the first part of his report in November 2012, no doubt required due to post-traumatic stress, having been assaulted by so many amnesiacs. We may only wonder if Dave ever remembers to publish the other two parts of Leveson's report.

Part 1: It's not easy being Dave

Dave inherited a mess, and he knew what to do - "build a bonfire with the party manifestos," he told Nick Clegg, "slash and burn that's our manifesto now, send for Iain Duncan Smith and tell him his time has come, drive out the scroungers, drive out the desperate and drive out the shameless...." suffice it to say, this was a private moment, that revealed Dave was not all the ticket. For good or ill, Dave now had a manifesto, his dander was up by golly, he wasn't one of Hugh Fearnley-Whittingstall's wretched dead fish, discarded by some crazy EU bureaucrat - he was the Captain of his very own Ship O'Fools.

Dave's 'Slash and Burn' manifesto was a short document; cull the underclass and privatise everything. The last item ticked along nicely, as more and more services have been farmed out to private contractors but there's still much to do on the culling issue. Confirmed in his belief that slash and burn is the only way forward, Dave persisted with the cuts agenda, even though it seemed the policy was causing much collateral damage throughout the land; Dave ignored the destitute, queuing for their soup and forged on.

Great Expectations

DIY Dave told us in his 2012 New Year's speech

"I know that if we lift our eyes to the other side we have it in our power to come through this stronger, better balanced, focused on what this fantastic country does best."

Dave's message was written by Edward Lear. What on earth was the man talking about, 'lifting his eyes to the other side'. What other side? What drugs were used to induce this acquisition of super-human new strength, balance, and focus.

Our focus, Dave tell's us, will be "on what this fantastic country does best." Now we knew, Dave had truly been on the Sherry over the Christmas break. Can this really be the same Dave who invented the phrase 'Broken Britain'. Hence forward, should we expect only to hear of Fantastic Britain.

Once upon a time all Dave's speeches told us how he was going to 'fix broken Britain', having returned from the other side, he was now going to change Britain. And where will this change occur?

"Brilliant and committed people work in public services", suffering at the hands of systemic failure; he'll change that. Expect more privatisation of the public sector, more outsourcing of local authority functions, more use of quangos and voluntary groups to direct the government's 'big society' pot hole repairs, litter picking, and grass cutting schemes. He told us, "we can turn these things around" i.e. City-boy excesses, tax dodging and welfare scrounging.

Dave also believes we can sell off a few more playing fields, provide more opportunities, raise aspirations and make our society more equal, and yes, we need a new quango to oversee progress.

Reshuffling the Pack

September 2012, Dave had seen the first half of his term in office pass him by. His achievements had been few, having surrounded himself by circus clowns like Jeremy Hunt, now promoted to steer the health service into waiting grasp of foreign multinationals. Clowns like Grant Shapps, charlatan, working class boy taken on all the trappings of the Bullingdon Club mind set, now promoted to lead the singing at Tory party gatherings.

In a sense Dave's reshuffle wasn't a pointless enterprise, it made sense within machinations of party politics, that is, within the fiasco of the Westminster Punch and Judy show but in terms of something much larger, more important, like social progress, it was pointless. Pointless because Dave and his ilk cannot think beyond the status quo; the belief that after a period of re-balancing the economy, culling the underclass, privatising education, health, and justice and yes, building another runway at Heathrow or Gatwick, then we will return to some virtuous growth path and all live happily ever after.

However, like a school boy, come back to halls after the hol's, Dave decided to start afresh, to reshuffle his Cabinet pack of clowns. The pundits said it was no big deal, not courageous, not Earth shattering. But perhaps, this was Dave's night of the long knives moment, shifting the Party to the Right, gearing up for the next election - without the Lib-Dems.

Old Duffer Ken Clarke was replaced by Chris Grayling as Justice Secretary but kept his seat at the Cabinet table, he didn't even notice that he'd lost his portfolio.

One of the numerous poison chalices was passed to Patrick McLoughlin, the new Transport Secretary, brought in to replace third runway doubter Justine Greening - she was moved to International Development and oblivion. McLoughlin has been a key player at the Tory casino for many years, like Shapps he's another working class traitor. No sooner had McLoughlin started playing with his new train set, the West Coast Mainline hit the buffers, i.e. the government's inability to run a simple rail franchise lottery.

Not a household name but Owen Paterson was asked to drive the tractor as Environment Secretary, you can find him most Sundays ploughing up the 'green belt' for recreation. Paterson hails from the same Bavarian beer halls as Iain Duncan Smith. Incidentally, Smith himself was not reshuffled, he thumbed his nose at new anti-squatting legislation and refused to move out of his office and Dave, weakly, backed down.

The five Lib-Dems at Dave's top table kept their jobs, no surprise there, these people had been more loyal to Dave than his Tory chums. Neither was it a surprise to see one of Dave's new team let him down at the first opportunity; Dave is just no good at picking winners. His new Chief Whip, Andrew Mitchell, was accused of telling police in Downing Street to fuck off and probably worse, he told them they were plebs. Mitchell denied everything, well, except the swearing bit, he eventually fell on a plastic sword and crawled off under a stone, the one recently vacated by David Laws. Mitchell must have realised his time was up during the Tory party conference, when the audience caught sight of his picture and booed.

Dave goes to Conference 2012

Now, his cabinet pack reshuffled, he was ready to reinvigorate the party faithful at Conference. His problem was that the party faithful didn't turn up, fifty per cent of the audience were either business men, lobbyists or young *apparatchiks*, there to network and promote their private sector solutions and, themselves.
Dave told Conference that there was only two options facing our nation, Sink or Swim. From whence he derived such optimism is unknown. Most of the passengers floating aimlessly aboard Dave's Ship O'Fools would consider sinking a blessing and with no where to swim to for sanctuary, the latter option was about as useful as a pledge from Nick Clegg. Captain Dave displayed incontrovertible evidence in the conference of his delusions, particularly so, when he announced that "Britain is on the right track."

Lunatic, on the right track and where pray were we bound for - this sort of talk doesn't fit with the nautical metaphor, surely he should have said on the right tack. Still, what should we expect from a man who surrounds himself with carpetbaggers and snake oil peddlers. Where's Henry the Navigator, where's Vasco da Gama, where are the people who know how to steer a ship. And just as the passengers aboard the Ship O'Fools were beginning to despair, Dave regained the tiller, telling The Telegraph "My job is to steer the ship in the right direction."

That very morning Dave had read the latest IMF report, telling him his economic plans were hopeless and worse, innumerate - the number crunchers at the Bank of England had been using the wrong multiplier to predict the impact of expenditure cuts on growth - the outlook was far grimmer than even Mervyn Micawber King could imagine. Deluded Dave, insisted we were on the right tack.... as the Rhyme of the Ancient Mariner passed through his brain.....

"Ah! Well a-day! What evil looks / Had I from old and young! / Instead of the cross, the albatross / About my neck was hung"

Anatomy of Madness

If Dave was not mad yet, it was only a matter of time until you would find him alongside Gordon Brown, selling the Big Issue in a shopping centre somewhere.

Cast your mind back to 2005, when he took on the leadership of the Tory party, full of confidence like the shampoo salesman of the year. The blue rinsers loved him, he had the right chemistry, or rather, the right chemical additives to match up to the King of the Angora Goats, Tony Blair. In opposition it was easy to maintain that unfazed, man of steel look, these days the look has turned into a manic stare.

Anyone seeking to understand madness might consider Foucault's masterly *History of Madness* (1961) but it might be easier to look at Dave's hopes and ambitions as they get trammelled by reality and then look harder, as he struggles to adapt to changing circumstances and begins to question his sense of self-belief. We all have doubting moments, just how many doubting moments does someone have to have before their outlook darkens? What triggers the gloom and sends a person reaching for the Valium?

Sailing the ship of state is not a solo endeavour, the captain relies on his chosen crew, perhaps it was the undeniable incompetence of so many of Dave's crew members that started the doubting.

A Case Demonic Possession

Dave, in a sense had been double whammied, continually let down by his crew and unintentionally possessed by a vacuous idea. Even the former Archbishop of Canterbury, Rowan Williams, described his Big Society as:

"aspirational waffle designed to conceal a deeply damaging withdrawal of the state from its responsibilities to the most vulnerable."

Not very comforting there from the Archbishop, he'd have been more use if he had offered exorcism to Dave.

Silly people

Dave has an uncanny knack of allowing elements on the loony fringe of the Tory party to grab some big headlines and by association this has made Dave look decidedly silly.

For example, in the area of Employment law reform, i.e. "compulsory no-fault dismissal", an idea stemming from a Government-commissioned report by venture capitalist Adrian Beecroft. The premise behind Beecroft's thinking is that employment laws, designed to protect workers' rights, are holding back the economy and need to be removed. Beecroft's report neatly sums up the Tory problem, i.e. the inability to distinguish between an asset and liability.

Lord Young, 78, Thatcherite to his core, was given a roving brief across Whitehall as Call Me Dave's enterprise tzar. The Lord's interests include music, book collecting, photography and talking bollocks. He told a journalist that during this "so-called recession the vast majority of people have never had it so good." He also said, "people will wonder what all the fuss was about". The Lord resigned. Well, that was back in November 2010 but 12 months later Lord Young silently returned as an advisor to Dave, on such matters as health and safety, that is, how to get round the legislation, to make things easier for jerry-builders. But H&S is not really the old duffer's main area of expertise. He's been providing Cabinet colleagues with a briefing on the benefits of a recession. Young's incisive analysis has led him to the conclusion that recessions are a good time to boost profits since the low wage conditions are a bonus for business.

Another of Dave's peers, Lord Bichard, suggested that people over retirement age should be required to do community work or lose some of their pension. According to Bichard "this would stop older people from being a "burden on the state". He also said, "so if you are old and you are not contributing in some way or another maybe there is some penalty attached to that." He never said what his social contribution would be before he dozed off again; we don't expect to hear from him anymore.

Peter Cruddas, Tory party treasurer, was caught out on camera telling undercover Times' reporters that he could arrange dinners with Cameron and Osborne for £250,000. Specifically, Cruddas's conversation with the reporters leaves you in little doubt that the Tory government can be bought, that anyone with enough cash can shape policy making. Having been caught out, Cruddas then resigned, making an idiot's apology, he said:

".... I deeply regret any impression of impropriety arising from my bluster in that conversation. Clearly there is no question of donors being able to influence policy or gain undue access to politicians."

Tory party central office knew nothing, Cameron knew nothing, Bertie Ahern knew nothing, the Daily Telegraph knew nothing. So, do we suppose that it was just Cruddas being silly?

Update: Cruddas July 2013

Cruddas won £180,000 libel damages from the Sunday Times allegations over financial irregularities in his management of party funds. He also received £500,000 in legal costs. Mr Justice Tugendhat said Mr Cruddas had "suffered public humiliation from the prime minister". However, we recall at the time, Mr Cameron felt fully justified in accepting Cruddas's resignation, describing his behaviour as unacceptable. And anyone who saw Cruddas showing off for the cameras would have to agree that his performance was unacceptable.

Foreign Secretary William Hague, always guaranteed to supply a silly soundbite said, at the unveiling of a statue of Ronnie Reagan in London....

"Statues bring us face to face with our heroes long after they are gone. President Reagan is without question a great American hero, one of America's finest sons and a giant of 20th century history. You may be sure that the people of London will take this statue to their hearts."

We think Hague meant just like the American populace took Ron's starring role in *Bedtime for Bonzo* to their heart.

The Silly Prize

However, George Osborne takes the prize for being the silliest person that Dave knows. At the beginning of April 2013, George somehow managed to connect up the murderous behaviour of Mick Philpott with the necessity for benefit cuts. Apparently, Philpott's benefit fuelled life-style was what the cuts to the welfare budget were all about, to stop underclass scum killing their children. Yes, said George, the Philpotts of this world must be put a stop to. Witless George was untroubled by the statistics, which attest to the fact, that a Philpott, like a Black Swan, is a rare event in Britain - even more rare than the collapse of the banking system. Suffice it to say, George was roundly condemned by everyone, except Captain Dave and the staff of the Daily Mail.

Let's remind ourselves that it was George who told us during 2011: "The time for banker bashing is over. We need to move on." In August 2014, HSBC announced it was setting aside a further £90m to pay back PPI claims. Lloyds announced it had put aside an additional £750 million to cover PPI, while RBS set aside an extra £250 million. Perhaps we should wait until the banks get honest before we move on.

George Osborne's mum and dad should ask St Paul's School for their money back.

Nick Hurd

Clearly Dave is fond of silly people who wear the same school tie as he does. Nick Hurd, 4th generation MP, cabinet minister for Civil Society, Eton, Oxford, and the Bullingdon Club is one such silly person.

In August 2013 he was asked to explain why there were 1.09 million young people, aged between 16 and 24 years out of work and not in education. Mr Hurd's response was to blame these young people for their circumstances:

"What we see in survey after survey is employers saying qualifications are important, but that just as important to us are so-called soft skills, character skills, the ability to get on with different people, to articulate yourself clearly, confidence, grit, self-control, these kind of qualifications and they are saying we are not seeing enough of them in kids coming out of schools."

All we know for sure about Mr Hurd is that he likes a survey that supports his jaundiced world view, i.e. one that allows him to blame the victims of Tory policies, rather than put forward some plans to remedy the situation. Making young people feel bad about themselves does not appear particularly bright.

Dave's Silly Moments

Also a cause for concern is Dave's habit of saying silly things before engaging his brain, e.g. saying that he would make the energy companies put homes on the lowest tariffs and saying that his government was going to be the greenest ever as he turns Britain into the fracking centre of the universe.

And one day, Dave may take a glum look back at his relationship with President Paul Kagame. He took a personal interest in increasing aid to Rwanda, which would have amounted to around £100m by 2015. He described Rwanda as "a role model for development and lifting people out of poverty in Africa". How could Dave have failed to notice that Kagame was running a repressive regime and using aid money to support armed insurgents, i.e. M23 in the Congo.

In truth, Dave doesn't think on his feet very well. In an interview with LBC back in 2006, he was asked what he thought of UKIP and he replied: "Ukip is sort of a bunch of ... fruitcakes and loonies and closet racists mostly." In November 2012 Dave's thoughtless comments came back to haunt him, after Rotherham Council removed children 'with ethnic backgrounds' from foster parents because they were members of UKIP and therefore unsuitable. A No.10 spokesman said "Mr Cameron did not say that all UKIP members were racist" - no, just most of them!

Now, the interesting point about the Rotherham case is that the Council objected to UKIP's stance of anti-multiculturalism. The Council is obviously not aware that Call Me Dave signalled the death knell for multiculturalism himself in February 2011, whilst outlining his anti-terror policy (you can see how all this fits together - can't you?). However, when you look in detail for the demon of multiculturalism it turns out to be a chimera. Another of Dave's silly moments, talking passionately about ridding the nation of a policy that was never there in the first place. Seek as hard as like you will not find any policy documents related to multiculturalism, nor will you find any relating to the assimilationist impulses of the majority group - the British do not have assimilationist impulses, they have football teams.

Perhaps, Dave's silliest moment occurred in March 2012, when tanker drivers were planning to strike and Dave told the nation not to panic, just top up their tanks - this led to queues for fuel across the nation and prices rose unaccountably since there was no tanker driver strike - the prices never did come down. (Update: petrol prices returned to pre-top-up-your-tank days around November 2014.)

Coming a close second on the silly moments list we saw Dave, following the announcement of a pasty tax, recounting, for assembled media lackeys, how he employed his finely tuned decision making skills on visiting a pasty shop - should he have a large or small pasty? Apparently, he says he opted for the large! The sight of the leader of the world's 6th wealthiest nation, a nation with many problems, talking bollocks about pasties signalled the end of hope. Until, that is, Ed Miliband and Ed Balls turned up in a Greggs to buy themselves some sausage rolls, just to let the world know they were the official opposition party - obviously, otherwise they would have been buying pasties. Let the record show that comedy is dead.

Dave had his brain completely disengaged when he came up with the genius idea of asking citizens which laws they would like to see gone. Well, if I told you that local authorities can draw on 1024 powers to gain access to your home, which ones would you choose to ditch? Would it be the one that allows snoopers to inspect your fridge to check its eco-friendly energy rating or to ensure 'illegal or unregulated hypnotism' is not taking place in your front room.

Examples like this demonstrate how absurd it was for the coalition to ask citizens which laws they would like to see repealed. How on earth are people supposed to know? New Labour introduced 400 of the 1024 powers in place, how many of these laws were citizens informed of and know about. The unregulated hypnotism scare originated in the 1950s and clearly the legislation needs to be reviewed now that the majority of citizens are mesmerised into a coma nightly by the awfulness of television output. However, should you wish to spend some time bringing yourself up to speed on UK legislation, do visit the government's latest new web site legislation.gov.uk. This site contains details of every law since 1267 - and the significance of that date is?

Note: 1267, Statute of Marlborough - introduced a raft of new laws to do with fly tipping - not much changes.

Disappointment

When the colleagues you surround yourself with can't be trusted and the world refuses to take your Big Idea seriously, you may be forgiven for seeking comfort from within the private realm. Perhaps turning to your chums from the Chipping Norton set, then, how much worse do you feel when they too turn out to be disloyal. How bad Dave must have felt nailing up the back door, to keep the Murdochs out, and burning all those photographs of the good times with Rebekah

Brooks, (now charged with conspiring to hack phones and perverting the course of justice alongside Coulson.. and how interesting to note how slow the legal process works. (Update June 2014: Brooks innocent, Coulson guilty, and that only cost you £40 million.)

Dave himself was being hounded in the Commons to reveal the email correspondence between himself, Brooks and Coulson, which he concealed from the Leveson enquiry. The emails are said to contain "embarrassing" exchanges. What form we wonder might this embarrassment take, might it perhaps reveal support for News Corps' controversial bid for control of BSkyB? Labour MP Chris Bryant estimates that 130 to 150 texts and emails held by No.10 were never sent to the Leveson Inquiry. Well, the texts finally emerged in November 2012, revealing nothing of interest, perhaps the illusive emails would be more fruitful? You'd think that Dave, in an effort to help his own inquiry, would have found the emails useful as an aide memoir since his failure to "recollect" at the Leveson inquiry was the very definition of embarrassing. (The emails will probably never see the light of day.)

U-turns and indecision

Deserted by Steve Hilton, Dave turned to top opinion pollster, Andrew Cooper. He cheered Dave up by telling him his three dozen U-turns were a good sign, i.e. they showed the government was listening to the people. Also, he pointed out, that Dave's U-turns had become so frequent that they were becoming commonplace, quite unremarkable, a normal part of modern politics and soon even the Guardian would stop writing about them.

The list of Dave's indecisive moments is a long one, as of October 2012, he had backtracked on 36 occasions. Not every climb down was a life changing moment, I mean, when he backed down over the destruction of buzzard nests at least he discovered that he had a Wildlife minister in the shape of Richard Benyon, a man who's never been heard or seen since?

Plans to sell 40,000 acres of state-owned woodland in England were abandoned. But there is still an intention to sell off around 15% of the original 40,000 acres. They are just going to be a bit quieter about it this time around.

Other moments have been more damaging, what was George Osborne thinking with the proposed 20% tax on pasties. Dave didn't have a clue about the ambient temperature of a pasty, he'd never eaten one in his life. Neither had Dave holidayed in a caravan but clearly a number of the coalition were members of the Caravan Club and Dave had a revolt on his hands after George talked about taxing static caravans.

Dave may well have been perturbed over pasties and caravans but his condition was made worse by George's plans to take child benefits away from core Tory voters, the aspiring middle income types. In response George watered down his plans. George had previously said that from January 2013 anyone earning above the 40 per cent tax rate threshold of £42,745 a year, would lose the benefit. Now he's going for a loss of benefits above £60,000 and a sliding scale of cuts between £50,000 and £60,000.

More U-turns in 2013

Dave's intention to introduce minimum alcohol pricing was shelved, apparently he now believed it was far too complicated.

And plain packaging for cigarettes would not go ahead but Dave denies that his new spin doctor in chief, Lynton Crosby, whose company does work for Philip Morris, influenced his decision to forget the idea.

Cameron's sloth on Lobbying

And does Dave really want to recall his big talk about cracking down on the lobbyists. All he's done is 'water down' proposals to clamp down on business and pressure groups seeking to unduly influence the political process. There may be a register of lobbyists but there will not be a code of conduct for lobbyists. We will not know how much these people are spending or who they are seeking to influence. The fact is that these people shouldn't be anywhere near the political process, they can have their vote like everyone else - once every five years. Or they can march through the streets with their banners, telling the world what they want, while they spend five hours in a police corral - proper democracy.

Note: The entire lobbying industry in the UK, estimated to be worth more than £2 billion a year, employs over 10,000 people; not bad for a subversive, anti-democratic enterprise.

Before the 2010 election Cameron promised he would shine "the light of transparency" on who was buying influence and power. Chloe Smith, the Cabinet Office minister in charge of future lobby industry legislation, has apparently not held any meetings with leading lobbyists since being given the job in 2011. A Bill for the recall of transgressing MPs was finally announced in the Queen's Speech 2014 but there was no news on a statutory code of conduct for MPs. Tory MP Zac Goldsmith says Dave's recall bill sounds grand enough but is only designed to dupe the public into thinking they can get rid of useless MPs. The reality, however, is that the equally useless Parliamentary Standards Committee, the same one that allowed Maria Miller to run rings round them, will decide what action is taken on transgressing MPs. Note: the Recall Bill has been postponed until after the 2015 election.

MPs do have Lord Nolan's Seven Principles of Public Life; selflessness, integrity, objectivity, accountability, openness, honesty, and leadership but it seems clear the poor man wasted his time.

Also, special interest All Party Parliamentary Groups, like Friends of Fiji are not required to publish minutes and accounts; or to provide details of the funding of APPG activities - although such action has been mooted.

All Party Parliamentary Groups (APPGs)

APPGs are semi-official groups of MPs and lords, which can be started by any parliamentarian who can muster enough cross-party signatures from both houses. While many serve as focus points for hobbies or campaign causes of MPs, they serve a dual function as a notorious back door for lobbyists, who can use them to fund drinks parties, overseas trips and more for big businesses and governments.

APPGs social clubs: parliament's choir is established as a group, as is its rowing team. As a result, many serve as avenues for sponsorship to come into the house.

The aforementioned choir, for example, received £65,000 in sponsorship from BT, while the rowing team receives £16,000 from Siemens towards the cost of parliament's boat race. Other groups get money from organisations even more closely tied to their interests: the APPG on beer, for example, exists to "promote the wholesomeness and enjoyment of beer and the unique role of the pub in UK society", and received £65,000 from the drinks industry for their efforts.

In all, there are now almost 600 such groups, representing countries, illnesses, industry and more – with some MPs enjoying membership of dozens at a time. The Guardian calculated more than £1.8m in outside sponsorship came into parliament via such all-party groups.

The weight of past lies

In the run-up to the 2010 election Dave made many promises which he turned his back on the moment he came to office. Some might say that he believed the things he said at the time but in the name of pragmatism he changed his mind. So that when he said that he would lead the "greenest government ever", some people might have believed that he was committed to environmental protection and a cleaner future. But then green turned to brown sludge when Dave endorsed fracking as the way forward for Britain's future energy needs. France has already banned fracking and the US are in denial over the human and environmental damage it's doing there. As the Americans like to say, fracking represents a clear and present danger, but Dave is prepared to take the risk on your behalf.

Three days before the 2010 election, Dave said on the BBC's Andrew Marr Show, "any cabinet minister" ... who comes to me and says 'Here are my plans' and they involve frontline reductions, they'll be sent straight back to their department to go away and think again". Yet £81bn in cuts are raining down on frontline services.

Would VAT rise? A month before the election, Cameron said: "Our plans involve cutting wasteful spending ... our plans don't involve an increase in VAT." VAT rose from 17.5% to 20%.

The Internet - Prior to the election Dave expressed his concerns. "Enough is enough. Our children are seeing too much, too young. If we want to make Britain a more family-friendly place to live – which is my passionate ambition – we have to take a stand. That's exactly what the Conservatives would do in government." Well, Dave had a chance to take a stand against the Internet Services Providers and he ducked the issue, ignored the parents, whom he asked to provide input and sided with the views of the Open Rights Group, a freedom of information lobby, oddly very keen to protect digital rights - odd because they can't see the irony.

Apart from grinding his teeth over Internet porn, Dave has been mainly silent on the disgrace of cared for children living in private care homes where they are treated like objects kept in a dark attic - not totally discarded, just out of sight and out of mind.

As for the NHS, "We will stop top-down reorganisations of the NHS," said the coalition agreement. The Lansley Act is all about top-down reorganisation. The coalition promised that "we will guarantee that health spending increases in real terms". The spending outturn for 2014/15 will see an increase of a mere 0.1%.

On Child benefit, Dave said, "I wouldn't change child benefit, I would not means test it, I don't think that's a good idea." He has.

On EMA, Michael Gove said, just before the election: "Ed Balls keeps saying that we are committed to scrapping EMA. I have never said this. We won't." He did!

On tax credits, the promise was to cut them only for families on £50,000, but the budget book shows families with an income of just £30,000 lose all credits.

Liam Fox promised "a bigger army for a safer Britain", but it's set to lose 11,000 soldiers.

We were also promised prison for anyone carrying a knife; no cuts to the navy; keeping the child trust fund for the poorest third of families; no hospital closures; 3,000 more midwives; – all lies, ditched we are told because Europe can't sort its problems out.

Dave's biggest lie

However, all of the foregoing, are as nothing to Dave's biggest lie; the need for all the cuts to the public sector, it's all simply costing too much, we can't afford it, we need reform, change, realism; austerity is the only solution, the party's over; the debt must be cut. The debt must be cut, otherwise the bond markets will start charging us unfavourable interest on our borrowing, why, well that's what lenders do, pick on someone in trouble and make their misery worse.

Interesting that for 200 of the past 250 years Britain has been in debt and seldom has this led to a national panic but Dave seems to view our current circumstances as worthy of a good panic. You see, it's not Dave's fault, it's the markets that are demanding austerity from everyone.

Professor Paul Krugman of Princeton University, says Dave has invented "invisible bond vigilantes" to justify his policies, but they "do not exist". Krugman on the contrary points out that bond markets are more likely to downgrade countries pursuing austerity, like Spain and Ireland because they are the least likely to pay their debt as they crash their economies.

Facing up to a hopeless situation is difficult and more so when your whole existence depends on it. Dave has pinned all his hopes on the success of his fiscal strategy and it's hard to be optimistic about the likelihood of success.

His cabinet team is weak and his leadership is also beginning to weaken, his alliance with the Lib-Dems is making him uncomfortable. There's simply not much to be upbeat about, the Olympics has come and gone and has been pretty much forgotten, so no more juice to squeeze there.

There's the worry over those emails being concealed from Leveson, and even more worry over the clown next door at No.11, what will he do next. (Answer, he will sell a house that the taxpayer paid for and walk away with a tidy £400,000 in the bank.) The number of u-turns have been a major embarrassment, and he continues to make a real dog's dinner of his dealings with Euroland.

It's not easy being Dave. But he doesn't make things easy for himself. Quite simply his judgment is flawed. His reaction to the cases of Andrew Mitchell and Peter Cruddas reveal this clearly, not enough time spent reflecting and too quick with the knee jerks. More darkly, we might also conclude that Dave is just a fair weather friend, who will not have your back when push comes to nudge.

The Poundland of Opportunity

Towards the end of 2012, Dave's legacy was beginning to take shape, with thoughtlessness at its core, driven by an obsession with growth, leaving social development to hope, osmosis, and the Chinese.

Dave's Poundland of Opportunity, across the whole piece, was still very much broken. And to add to Dave's woes, Mumsnet had it in for him, saying he's elitist, too posh, and "out of touch". In a poll carried out for Mumsnet by Ipsos Mori, 42% of all women said they would vote for Labour, compared with just 29% who would back the Tories. However, the Mumsnet assault is not uppermost on Dave's mind, its background noise, too much background noise.

Dave reflected on the problems with his flagship welfare policies and the increasingly dysfunctional operation of the Bavarian wing of the party over at the Department for Work and Pensions.

First the national roll out of the Universal Credit scheme was scaled down to no more than a mini pilot and now the scheduled transition from the Disability Living Allowance to Personal Independence Payments is being held up. Computer systems failure again, it seems they can't even buy in the technical expertise to deliver the goods. Or more likely, the systems are so poorly specified by civil servants, who simply do not have the expertise to draw up workable plans, and are not given the necessary time by ministers like Iain Duncan Smith, striving for recognition before they get airbrushed out of the picture.

Somewhere amid all this chaos people's lives were being trammelled and all Iain Duncan Smith does is defend his department's failed policies; The Work Programme, totally ineffective and costly; the Atos Healthcare assessments found wanting in all regards, and deadly.

Conference 2013

At the 2013 Tory Conference Dave told his audience that the Conservative plan was to build a Land of Opportunity. He told his audience this 17 times but had trouble describing this mythical land. Three years earlier Dave was going to build the Big Society, the new Camelot from the ruins left by New Labour but Dave was unable to explain that vision. That's the thing with visionaries, they have a problem explaining the detail.

Apart from the lack of detail at conference, Dave appeared to be moving even further away from his grasp on reality. The following statement from his conference speech seems to provide us with more evidence of Dave's delusions:

"We're spending up to £14,000 on one individual to get them into work – and already almost 700,000 people have got onto the Work Programme."

So let's be clear, it's costing £14,000 to place each individual in a job through the Work Programme. That might be money well spent if the Programme was not a cataclysmic failure in the core area of finding people work. The fact is the private companies that Dave has employed to find people work are no good at it and they couldn't care less because they know that the government will cover up their failings. And let's be clear, when Dave says "...700,000 people have got onto the Work Programme.", he's being totally disingenuous. He makes it sound like these people have achieved something, they have succeeded by gaining access to the Programme - this is complete garbage. Unemployed people do not aspire to join the Programme, they have no choice.

Dave's 'to don't' list

Many people function using a 'to do list', Dave has a 'to don't' list, things he would rather forget about 2013. Like the opposition to HS2 and skepticism surrounding its supposed economic benefits. Like the dysfunctional performance of Theresa May's Home Office in its handling of illegal immigration, the disaster of the 'go home vans' and he really does not want to think about all those Roma gypsies that no one knew were here and all those Bulgarians that will be joining them. The costs of the Trident replacement and the associated complications of Scottish independence. GCHQ's cooperative snooping antics with the NSA, all too embarrassing now it's in the public domain. Gove's manic and hopeless educational reforms, the man just has no grasp of history. And the press, Dave really does not want to think about how to deal with the press post-Leveson.

From Broken Britain to Moral Collapse

It's January 2014, Dave reflects, hopefully. Dave is hopeful, that with May 7, 2015 in sight that citizens' expectations have been suitably adjusted and they are now fully accepting of the need for austerity and that they have not been able to keep pace with all the policy measures taken to make their lives better. The glorious thing about people who can't keep up is that they are likely to get lost in the detail and more than likely, they will cover up their lack of understanding by agreeing with everything - or convince themselves that nothing is actually happening anyway.

The flood waters are lapping and the government's response has been found wanting. In fact, there's a lot of want when it comes to government policy. Flagship education reform, i.e. 'free schools', is in trouble, poor Ofsted reports and school closures. NHS reforms like the new non-emergency 111 phone line has created massive problems for A&E departments and ambulance services. Energy policy is shambolic and being challenged by the EU. The police service is revealing itself as the enemy within. Mark Carney at the BoE is looking more confused than even Mervyn King managed in all those years in charge. And the unintended consequences of the party's Kafkaesque welfare reforms make the coalition look more nasty as the days go by and worse, silly.

Colleagues causing concern, Dave takes stock

Dave is ruefully reviewing the relationship with the Lib-Dems and is hopeful that casting them adrift will be easier next year due to their ridiculous antics in relation to Lord Rennard's behaviour, with the strident denials of accused sex pest Nick Hancock contributing to a glorious Lib-Dem own goal. The slothlike intervention of Zombie party leader, Nick Clegg, did little to inspire. At least Dave can rely on the Lib-Dems to wander the land aimlessly.

He does not have the same confidence that he can rely on his colleagues to stay out of trouble. Phillip Hammond, at the MoD, has made a mess of things and that lot over at Defra are definitely a cause for concern, Owen Paterson certainly knew when to pull a sicky. But let's hope no one stops to ask who put Eric Pickles in as a replacement. Visiting the submerged Somerset Levels, one day he said the experts at the Environment Agency were a bunch of blunderers and next day in parliament, he said what a marvellous job they were doing. There is a suggestion that Pickles could have played a major role in flood defences - by doubling as a sandbag!

Dave was also slightly peeved that those clowns over at GCHQ had not managed to keep their snooping antics secret. After all, they are supposed to be operating covertly, not on the front page of the Guardian. Citizens are not supposed to know about things like Dishfire and Prism and what on earth are we going to do with two million text messages a day. Next they will be asking for more storage and bigger computers, this war on terror is getting expensive.

And what was Vince Cable up to over at the Business Department, everyone knows he sold off the Royal Mail on the cheap and then allowed vested interests to make a killing. Cable trusted Goldman Sachs, USB and others for a princely sum, to set the offer price, (that would be the same Goldman Sachs who said Greece was good to go - sound finances and all that - when it was allowed to join the European Union). Vince Cable and Co. have not apologised for making such a mess of the sale of Royal Mail and the companies paid £17m to handle the sale told a select committee that they did a good job and the 330p price was correct. And yet a few days later, Goldman Sachs was telling its investors that the price would settle at 600p. Then they said that by the year's end 700p would not be unrealistic. Vince continued to claim that he did a good job. Vince's main advisors on the sell off were Lazard's Financial Advisory, a company not renowned for advising on public sell offs. However, we do know that Lazard's Asset Management bought itself a bundle of Royal Mail shares and made a killing of around £8m. Lazard's would like everyone to know that its two companies are completely separate legal entities, so any talk of inappropriate behaviour and conflicts of interest is just wrong.

HS2 Limited are definitely high on Dave's cause for concern list, the company running the high speed rail project, that few seem to want, have spent £300m over the past three years. All this spending has taken place before a shovel has been put in the ground and before parliamentary approval has been given for the scheme to go ahead. Looking at an itemised list of HS2 Ltd's spending it looks like the children have been let lose in a sweetshop. Much of the spending has gone to propaganda and support for all and any parties allying themselves with the project, so, lots of spending on beanos, and consultants and lawyers. The waste of money here even extended to paying pollsters Ipsos Mori £500,000 to gather intelligence on the effects of the rail line on 'blighted' areas.

So much is happening at the NHS, it's hard for Dave to keep up. Dave has been impressed by Hunt's hands on approach, he's been phoning up hospitals, telling them he heard a bedpan drop and wanted an explanation. Perhaps someone should ask Hunt if he has nothing more pressing to focus on. Like his new non-emergency helpline, 111, which has created an adverse reaction among citizens, i.e. the new propensity for people in distress to go directly to A&E departments rather than waste their time discussing their condition with a call centre chimpanzee. The consequence of this marvellous initiative has meant ambulances parked up for hours with patients on board, unable to unload due to overcrowding caused by the 111 dodgers, with the knock on effect that fewer ambulances are then available to deal with emergency calls.

Dave is also pondering the Home Office and Theresa May's stewardship. The poor woman just does not have a handle on her job. If it wasn't for Channel 4's Dispatches programme she wouldn't know what was going on, thousands of illegals waving their phoney certificates, got from agencies legitimised by May's own department. And Dave's just hoping the public have forgotten the Abu Qatada fiasco and those silly 'Go Home' vans.

Talking of forgetting, some dark corner of Dave's mind has just reminded him that he was going to do away with all those silly targets being applied to the NHS. He knows that some targets were scrapped, only to be replaced by new ones, with financial penalties attached. Over the past year this system of penalties cost hospitals £390m, i.e. funding that has been withheld. NHS England claims that it's diverting funds into quality care beyond hospitals - that's another part of Dave's cunning plan for the nation's health, provide preventative care in the community. You know, like Drop in Centres that tell you to get lost when you do.

Dave was able to express a sigh of relief when Maria Miller asked to borrow the Party's plastic sword and promptly fell on it, whilst mumbling something about being a "distraction". All very odd because the public were unaware of her existence until they discovered she was an expenses fiddler and an arrogant person to boot.

So, undistracted, the great British public were able to give their full attention to some good news on the economy. Those bean counters at the IMF were saying that the UK was the fastest growing economy across Europe. A critical person might be tempted to point out that most of Europe has got one foot in the grave, so outpacing the moribund was no great achievement - although Dave and his boy George did manage to make it seem rather grand. However, since they never tire of telling us how central Europe is to Britain's economic wellbeing there is not much to be complacent about. Across the whole of Euroland inflation is below the 2% target rate and at least nine countries have gone into deflation and are being told to start printing money to solve the problem.

Behind the scenes Dave was busy replacing the 'placemen' at the top of all the commissions and quangos that really manage things day to day. He decided to let Lady Morgan, chair of Ofsted go but the lady did not go quietly, pointing the finger at Dave for getting rid of her and noting that Dave had recently put Tory supporters in charge of the Charity Commission and Arts Council. Agencies like these are crucial in terms of the struggle for hearts and minds, propaganda is the name of the game and these agencies are funded handsomely to promote the Tory message. Interesting to note that the Commission that was responsible for hiring the quango elite has been quietly disappeared by this government.

The decision not to reappoint Lady Morgan is significant since Ofsted has been turning into the dog that eats its owner. Civitas, the think tank established by Michael Gove, was very critical of Sir Michael Wilshire, Ofsted's chief inspector, following his criticism of Gove's pet 'free schools' scheme. Civitas accused Ofsted of stifling innovation and said it should lose its powers to judge free schools and academies. In keeping with its libertarian leanings, Civitas believes that free schools and academies should assess their own performance. Well, what Civitas actually said was that a new inspection service should be set up, one that understands the innovative ethos of free schools. All those Ofsted inspectors are just stuck in a bygone age of 1960's pupil-centred malarkey.

Cyril Smith: Unfinished business

During any government regime the ghosts and misdeeds of the past may come back to haunt the present. The cover up by the establishment for decades of Cyril Smith's disgusting molestation of small children may superficially have nothing to do with Dave and his government. However, when we learn that the Cabinet Office blocked FoI requests for information concerning who put Smith forward for a knighthood, we may wonder why? Eventually they gave up the name, it was David Steel.

Newspaper men managed to track down Steel to the hobbit hole where he now lives, from there he described Smith's nastiness as 'ancient' and after all Smith was in the Labour Party when he was busy disciplining young boys in Rochdale, so his activities had nothing to do with the Zombies. Steel still had his 1979 copy of Private Eye and had even re-read it for his interview. That's it, that's as proactive as he was prepared to be - all too much trouble for an ageing hobbit?

We suggest that Steel broadens his reading to include a publication from 2014, i.e.

Smile For The Camera: The Double Life of Cyril Smith by Simon Danczuk and Matthew Baker

And something for Steel to think about, use of the word ancient, to chase away demons from the past will not wash; we may not be able to easily find the bodies but we can still smell the stench of wrong doing.

The thing about Liberals and public school types in general is that they do not see much wrong with a bit of spanking. Least ways this was how Liberal leader David Steel viewed the handy work of paedophile Cyril Smith, yes, Mr Clean laughed off the vile behaviour of Smith. Many knew Smith was a nasty piece of work, a beast who would be most comfortable in Jimmy Savile's mobile home and yet they all turned a blind eye, the police had enough evidence to arrest Smith but all the evidence was hidden from the public gaze.

Interestingly, none of the national newspapers ever wrote about Smith creeping around the corridors of boys homes in the dark. Someone high up the food chain was covering up for Smith, perhaps that someone was part of the same paedo' gang. Towards the end of 2014 we learnt that at least two newspapers were threatened with D-notices over printing anything about paedophile rings among the establishment. The people responsible for issuing D-notices tell us today that they have no evidence that this action was taken to prevent the publication of revelations.

Current Lib-Dem leader and deputy Prime Minister, Nick Clegg told us in 2012, after Smith's behaviour 'officially' came out of the shadows:

"I am deeply shocked and horrified by these terrible allegations and my thoughts are with the victims who had the courage to speak out."

That was the same Nick Clegg who led the cheer leading for Smith when he left politics, telling the world what a

41

marvellous chap he was and what a great contribution he made to the party. More recently Clegg was at pains to distance himself from the taint of Smith, claiming it was all so long ago for him to know anything. Some critics pointed out that he would have had more credence as a leader if he declared an intention to launch a party led inquiry, and root out and name anyone who covered up for Smith. No, not Nick, he just wants to forget the whole thing.

Historic child sex abuse

It appears as if Nick Clegg is not the only one who would like to forget the past or put otherwise, some people might be seeking to pretend they were not there when the pin-striped buggers were hoping in and out of bed with little boys down at the Elm Guest House, in Barnes, West London.

A journalist from the Exaro website tipped off MP Tom Watson that something rotten had gone on and a number establishment figures were involved. This prompted Watson to ask Dave at Prime Minister's Question time what he thought about it all. Um, next we learn that Operation Fairbank is under way, a secret police investigation, this morphs into Operation Fernbridge, an open criminal investigation - don't hold your breath, you'll expire.

We learnt that back in 1983, MP Geoffrey Dickens gave a dossier on the child abuses to then Home Secretary, Leon Brittan, Brittan gave it to someone else and they lost it. Who lost it? Was it the police, was it the Home Office, was it the cleaner - who knows?

Simon Danczuk MP had been tracking the stench of Cyril Smith for some time and by 2014 he had connected him to the Elm Tree Guest House. It was all too much for Dave, he told May to get an inquiry in place - that's where he hit a brick wall. Ms May seemed unable to choose an appropriate chair person for the inquiry. She called on Lady Butler-Sloss, no good, too close to the events of yesteryear, then she called on Fiona Woolf, no good, neighbours with the Brittans'. How far would the Home Secretary have to go, that is travel, to find an individual without any personal interest in this inquiry.

There's only one certainty in all this, the victims of child sexual abuse are not happy with May and they do not trust this government to deliver a genuinely independent inquiry that brings the buggers face to face with their hideousness and hands out suitable punishment. However, they say this new inquiry will be of the Hillsborough type, we think that means it will drag on for years and the victims will eventually extract the truth like a rotten tooth, only to find the diseased root has been left in.

Muddying the waters

Back in 2013, the Home Office commissioned a review into how it handled abuse allegations between 1979 and 1999. Quite what it reviewed is uncertain since over hundred documents relating to sex abuse had been 'lost or destroyed'. In July 2014, Peter Wanless, boss of the NSPCC, was asked by Theresa May to review the Home Office review, as well as, how police and prosecutors responded to complaints. The upshot, Wanless found nothing because there was nothing to be found, that is, he could not find any of the 'lost' documents. The point of the Wanless Review may be lost on many people but perhaps he might like to consider a review into how the NSPCC responded to child sex abuse victims of the Westminster buggers between 1979 and 1999? It is almost as if someone is trying to persuade the historic child sex abuse inquiry, still without a chair person , that there's no point in focussing on the Home Office because they do not know anything.

The IPCC takes a hand

It would be nice to hear what the man on the Clapham Omnibus made of the Wanless review and to know whether that man was able to disentangle the announcement that the Independent Police Complaints Commission is to investigate how three police forces dealt with information about paedophiles supplied by Canadian police. This investigation is about to happen because the Essex, North Wales and North Yorkshire police did not deal in a timely or urgent manner with the information supplied. And our own version of the FBI, the National Crime Agency have already apologised for their sloth.

The IPCC says it takes the abuse of children seriously, that's reassuring. However, this investigation has nothing to do with historic child sex abuse by establishment figures. We already know that the police have an appalling track record in sex abuse cases. The IPCC action is apparently driven by "considerable public concern about how the police deal with sexual offences involving children". The man on the omnibus may well conclude that there is a connection between Wanless and this investigation, both are designed to reassure the public that something is being done - straight from the first page of the Cynics Handbook, 'being seen to be doing something' may be confused with purposeful action and is therefore highly desirable.

Dave gets religion...

Dave said the UK is a Christian country "and we should not be afraid to say so". Well, statistically he's wrong. We learn from the British Social Attitudes survey, carried out annually by the National Centre for Social Research, that we are a less-religious country, with 51% describing themselves as non-religious and 43% as Christian.

The UK does however have an established church that's past its sell by date and that church is unhappy with Dave's policies in relation to the poor. Dave addressed an audience of churchman in Oxford and was at pains to assert his own Christian credentials. He called for a revival of traditional Christian values to counter Britain's "moral collapse". Not only is Britain broken, it is also suffering from moral collapse? Can we detect a holistic purpose from Dave here, fixing the body and the soul of the nation.

Some may view Dave's praise for Christian values as a cynical attempt to placate an increasingly critical Anglican church, that has finally woken from eons of slumber to champion the plight of the down trodden. The proliferation of food banks are bad press for Dave and easy meat for his critics and the situation is made worse by Iain Duncan Smith, talking nonsense about 'supply creating its own demand' in relation to food banks. Well, of course, Iain, there would be no food poverty if the food banks did not exist - we get it. (Duncan Smith apparently lied about his academic qualifications during his rise to the top, he would struggle to conceal his lacklustre intellect today.)

Duncan Smith expresses one strand of Tory thinking on the rise of food banks, another attempts to command higher moral ground, by claiming that the existence of food banks demonstrates the generosity of the British populace, no doubt inspired by those Christian values. Choose either view and you have neatly dodged reality, that is, the reality of the economic inequality that signifies Great Britain. Duncan Smith seeks to deny the issue and Christians' placate their consciences by turning the spectacle of food banks into some kind of national triumph to be celebrated. Indeed, Isobel Hardman, writing in the Spectator told us that food banks are a sign of the strength of Britain's social structure. Isobel is also at pains to assure us that they are not a symptom of poverty, they are a response to a host of social ills, there are abused women, families stricken with debt problems or overwhelmed in the holidays when there are no free school meals to tide them over. She also acknowledges that some people may be there due to low pay and problems with Duncan Smith's benefits reforms.

Horizon Scanning Programme

Dave has been busy blowing out the candle on the Horizon Scanning Programme birthday cake, it is now 12 months old. Although, he might not have been that pleased with the programme's scanning efforts - nothing, that is, nothing worth reporting. The idea behind this so-called programme is to peer into the future in an effort to figure out what may happen by way of threats, risks and opportunities.

A Commons committee looking at the lack of output stemming from this programme has concluded that it has "substantial weaknesses", is not using the expertise of external experts and that there was a "worrying lack of clarity" about what the programme was about.

The committee was also not impressed that the baton of ministerial oversight for the programme was passed after only six months from Francis Maude to Oliver Letwin. Some ministers are useless and some are less useful, both Maude and Letwin would fall under the the latter heading. One created a fuel panic single-handedly and the other decided to use the waste bins of St. James's Park to dispose of official documents.

The committee was reassured by Letwin:

"We have not been as quick to publish as we would have liked but we are taking time to do the work carefully and we are set to publish a number of papers later this year on gov.uk."

Dave's interest in future gazing is quite amazing and contradictory, given his earlier adherence to the ideas of Nassim Taleb.

The banking crisis was a rare event, what Dave calls a Black Swan event, i.e. something big that happens and that you can't predict. Well, at least that's what Dave's guru, Nassim Taleb says. In his spare time Dave can be found sat crosslegged at the feet of his guru Nassim.

In these rare moments, Nassim will tell Dave tales of Black Swans, themselves rare, almost as rare as a Windows operating system that works (in my experience). Nassim will probably be reading from his book *'The Black Swan'* and Dave will be all ears like a rabbit, with big eyes like a panda on the look out for ideas, to use in his Big Society. Dave is always on the look out for new ideas.

For Nassim, Big is bad. Dave makes a note to tell Willetts to find another word. Big, Nassim says, makes a mess of running things. Random is also bad because randomness encourages people to think they can predict the future. Well, Nassim says they can't because they don't know enough.

Nassim's message is that Black Swans are like unknown unknowns - not very helpful then? The point is that Dave imagines that he has his finger on what's hot, on cutting edge ideas, new ways of thinking about problems and is not afraid to use those ideas in his policies. For instance, David (two brains) Willetts, the Minister of State for Universities and Science and Space, tells us, "There's a very close link between *black swan thinking* and what we're doing on health or education." It doesn't matter if you don't understand what Willetts means - Dave will know.

Readers note: writing convention suggests that only foreign words and book titles should be italicized, however, when government ministers use phrases like *black swan thinking* it is permissible to assume they are talking a language other than English.

The Rise of the Loonies

Dave is now going through a period of listening and learning, no not like GCHQ. Dave has been stunned by the success of UKIP in the May EU and local elections. His deputy, Nick Clegg is spending much of his time on eBay, searching for a brave face to wear. The Euro elections went badly for Nick, his party were mauled savagely by the electorate, pushed into fifth place behind the Green Party, retaining only one of its 12 MEPs. The LibDems also lost 72% of the council seats they were defending. These elections were all about the rise of UKIP, whom Dave stupidly once referred to as loonies. Even more stupid, some Tory MPs said that the UKIP vote was a protest vote, this did not sit well with the electorate hence Dave's talk of 'listening and learning'. You know, responding to the electorate's concerns, the way politicians rarely do.

Unfazed Nick told the world:

"He was proud of having taken on UKIP and stood up for the values that we believe in", even though, he said, "it didn't work".

Some in the party were calling for Nick to stand down as leader, that clamour grew louder following the Newark by-election, where the Lib-Dems lost their deposit. UKIP came second in Newark, pushing Labour into third place. This by-election came about following the resignation of Patrick Mercer, who quit over a cash-for-questions scandal. The Tories won the seat but had their majority slashed by 8000 but Dave spun that into a success story - muttering something about the vote being a strong endorsement of Tory economic policy. In reality Dave won the day by flooding Newark with 1000 activists working for their candidate, he visited the constituency four times himself and many of his key ministers also played their part. When it comes to the general election the resources will just not be there for this kind of blanket canvassing.

Also the defection of some Tories to UKIP is looking more likely as Dave dithers over Europe. Douglas Carswell jumped ship at the end of August 2014. How many more will follow him to the UKIP camp. Dave called Carswell's departure "regrettable".

The Trojan Horse Saga

A letter, alleging that Islamists were taking over schools in Birmingham, now said to be a hoax, led to a panic tantamount to that of the Zinoviev letter during the General Election of

1924, that too was a hoax but it destroyed the credibility of the moderately socialist Labour Party. The Home Secretary Theresa May blamed Michael Gove for not dealing with the Jihadi governors who were taking control these schools, claiming his department had known for years that so-called Islamisation was taking place but did nothing about it. Gove retorted that terrorism and extremism and such were matters for the Home Office not the education department. Ms May's special adviser struck back by publishing internal correspondence from May to Gove on the Home Office website criticizing Gove, she was sacked. Dave took a hand, Gove apologised to May, both were left looking less than grown up.

Meanwhile Ofsted released reports on 21 Birmingham schools, its shock troops had been sent in to root out the Jihadis. Ofsted boss, Sir Michael Wilshaw, said "a culture of fear and intimidation has taken grip" in some schools. Six schools were put into special measures, most necessary apparently because when schools are in the grip of fear then extreme views might emerge. Underlying this message is the assumption that extreme views may become terrorist acts, so best to nip the views in the bud before they blossom.

But the Trojan Horse letter has done more than create a panic over the subversion of the education process by extremists, it has created an imponderable debate over the nature of Britishness. Dave himself is clear about British values and wants all schools in the land to be teaching them, well at least he thinks he's clear. He said:

"The values I'm talking about – a belief in freedom, democracy, tolerance of others, accepting personal and social responsibility, respecting and upholding the rule of law – are the things we should try to live by every day."

In truth there's nothing uniquely British about any of that. We may agree that a radical Muslim promoting Sharia Law is in the wrong country but we have to sound a note of caution when 95% of a given community follow Islam that parents may develop expectations that diverge from the mainstream of British beliefs. Dave now seems to be saying to these parents you must 'get British or else'. Well, that doesn't sound very British. From the start of the new school year expect all schools throughout the land to have a nice new folder entitled "Teaching British Values".

Dave tried to save his inability to define British values by invoking the spectre of the 13th century Magna Carta as something for all good Britains to celebrate; safe ground really, the peasants didn't read it then and are unlikely to do so now.

One of Mr Gove's acolytes, Dominic Cummings, unkindly suggested that Dave had "no sense of purpose" about what he wants to achieve in government. He also said:

"As Bismarck said about Napoleon III, Cameron is a sphinx without a riddle. Everyone is trying to find the secret of David Cameron, but he is exactly what he appears to be. There's no mystery to him. He had a picture of Macmillan on his wall … That's all you need to know."

Well, there is one small extra detail we would like to clear up - what on earth is Cummings talking about? There is no secret to Dave, he's a Blair clone, all presentation over substance. Perhaps the mention of Macmillan is an obscure reference to Macmillan's 'night of the long knives', when he ruthlessly reshuffled everyone he didn't like. Now, can you imagine Dave doing that?

Before getting into No.10 gave promised that at least one third of Tory shortlisted candidates would be women. He seems to have realised that he is way off the target he set himself. So he decided to allow more to board his Ship O' Fools.

His memory may have been jogged by criticism, some time back, from the opposition about the lack of females on his front bench. Perhaps he thinks that the female electorate will be elated by this move or it may be a vain attempt to make Cabinet meetings look less like a Bullingdon Club get-to-together.

However, one change that took the press pack by surprise was the demotion Mr Gove from Education Secretary to Chief Whip and replacing him with the unknown Nicky Morgan. This is a change he should have made a year ago, if he's expecting voters to forget Gove's disregard for the teaching profession.

The most surprising change, however, must be the appointment of Philip Hammond to foreign secretary; Michael Fallon replaced him as defence secretary. Over the past four years Hammond has been hopping around the departments like a frog. As transport secretary he told us that HS2 would bring a revolution in rail transport on a par with the coming of the railway in the 19th Century. As defence secretary he told us that building an aircraft carrier without any planes was cause for celebration. Now, we must wait in anticipation for more earth shattering pronouncements in his new role. We only hope he does not think that saying "unacceptable" at every turn of events like his predecessor William Hague is all the job requires.

Fast track anti-terror legislation

In a hardly democratic piece of trickery, the government proposed to rush through DRIP, the Data Retention and Investigatory Powers Bill. The Bill has a sunset clause, meaning it is supposedly temporary, expiring on 31 December 2016.

The back story here is simple. The European court of justice overturned the European data retention directive on 8 April 2014. Thereby making the government's current snooping activities illegal, certainly of no value in a court of law. Solution, introduce national legislation that makes your wrong doing legal.

The purpose of data retention is for investigating serious crimes, not for investigating the whole population but that's what it will be used for.

And take note, this legislation is not just a carbon copy of the now outlawed EU directive. DRIP contains new and unprecedented powers, according to the Guardian "for the UK to require overseas companies to comply with interception warrants and communications data acquisition requests and build interception capabilities into their products and infrastructure". How long will it be before Dave introduces our very own Patriots' Act?

Out of touch in Europe

Most people arm themselves with a Rough Guide before venturing across the channel, not Dave. Dave pledged to stop the eurozone using the European courts and Brussels institutions to uphold its own breakaway fiscal pact being set up outside the EU treaty. This one is odd, it's as if Dave thought he had a veto but no one in the EU cared, so he decided not to use his veto? Dave's behaviour in Europe has been described as "picking a fight in an empty room" then leaving, claiming to be the victor.

He also believed he could veto the euro budget rise for the coming years. Dave wanted a freeze but he lost a vote in Parliament on the issue at the end of October 2012. Tory backbench rebels joined Labour and refused to accept anything less than a budget cut.

Well, Dave went to discuss the budget with the other 26 countries and nothing happened, they met again in January 2013. And big Dave managed to get us a rebate of some £29bn (mainly due to German support) but alas due to complex rebate rules we will still end up paying more for our membership card.

Is Dave confused on Europe, Europeans seem a trifle confused over what it is he's seeking, when he speaks of 're-negotiating' treaties. Dave has promised the British public an in-out referendum on EU membership in 2017. Before we get there, he wants to re-negotiate Britain's terms of membership. However, the view is that he has no chance. What exactly does he want, he speaks of a more 'competitive and flexible' arrangement but the likes of Martin Schulz, European parliament president, says that re-writing EU treaties is wishful thinking and François Hollande says that re-writing is not top of anyone else's agenda. Meaning that there's no appetite for allowing individual countries to cherry pick treaties, allowing bespoke agreements. Straightforwardly, Britain is either all in or all out.

Meanwhile Dave was fast losing favour with other euro leaders over the impending 'choosing' of the president of the European Commission, arguably the top job in the EU. The 'chosen one' this time around is hardline federalist Jean-Claude Juncker. Dave's unhappy:

"I want to to set out the UK position on the issue and to be clear about our longer- term vision for the European Union. Voters sent a clear message at the European elections (May 2014). They are disillusioned with the way Europe is working. They are demanding change so it focuses on what they care about: growth and jobs."

As far as Dave was concerned, Mr Juncker was unlikely to be very responsive to any calls to unpick the federalist agenda. At root Dave's angst stemmed from being left out of the Juncker choosing and when he complained to Mrs Merkel, she told him to get lost. Dave does have a point about the choosing of Juncker, it came about as a part of a horse trading process in the European Parliament, a process that was never agreed by national parliaments? Perhaps we do need a referendum. Dave's swan song on the Juncker choosing was to try and force the other leaders to vote on the issue. Dave never did explain the purpose of voting on an issue where the outcome had already been decided - well, they had a vote anyway, 26 to 2 in favour of Juncker.

The Polish Foreign Minister, Radek Sikorski, summed up Dave's position:

"... Mr Cameron fucked up the 2011 EU fiscal compact on budget discipline, which the UK tried to block. Because he's not interested, because he doesn't get it, because he believes in this stupid propaganda, he stupidly tries to manipulate the system". (Wprost magazine, June 2014)

In sum: Dave wants to resist the federalist agenda for Europe, he's not winning, he wants to re-negotiate bits of the Treaty, no one is interested, he didn't want Juncker for Commission president, no one was listening.

Before we move on let us re-echo what Dave says voters want. He says they want change that focuses on jobs and growth. How wrong can one man be? What the British public want is for someone to tell them what the point of the EU is but a good starting point would be for Dave to spell out clearly what it is he wants to renegotiate and why? And while he's in explanation mode, he can tell us who Lord Hill of Oareford is, i.e. the person he has selected to be the UK's European Commissioner for the next five years. On second thoughts, perhaps an unelected lord is the right person for a job in the anti-democratic chamber of euro commissioners.

More Background Noise

Background noise in Dave's world refers to the things he has no control over, like the silly behaviour of his colleagues and more so, press stories that reveal some unpalatable facts about life in Dave's Big Society.

An 83-year-old man was arrested and banned from seeing his wife for trying to alleviate her suffering by applying a pain relief patch to her leg. The man had been her only carer for 15 years, but when her dementia got worse she entered Allendale Residential Home, in Manchester.

When staff discovered the patch contained morphine, they contacted the police. Four days later, the man was arrested on suspicion of 'administering a noxious substance'. And thus began a saga of amazing stupidity, by police, social workers and care workers - the process became more important than the people involved.

His house was searched; he was locked up in a cell for seven hours without anything to eat; he was fingerprinted and forced to give a DNA swab. It was midnight before he was interviewed, eventually being bailed in the early hours of the morning. And as part of his bail conditions, he was barred from contacting his wife, this was subsequently changed to only seeing his wife with supervision. After two months of investigating the police decided to take no action.

All this nonsense took two months because the case was passed to the specialist Greater Manchester Police Public Protection Investigation Unit. The case became a 'multi-agency strategy' operation. The police justified their activity thus: "This was a potentially serious incident in which a vulnerable elderly woman with significant health issues could have come to serious harm. " It would appear that harm is assured for anyone who falls foul of the Public Protection Investigation Unit.

Dave goes to Conference
For the last time?

Dave went to the Tory conference having lost another MP to the Loonies. Mark Reckless, who apparently was not a loyal party member, jumped ship on the eve of conference and was last seen having a pint with Nigel Farage. True to form Tory bile boiled over, no doubt Dave's Baldricks were briefing that the best way to handle the defection was by denigrating Mr Reckless's character. Well, the man must have multiple character flaws to pursue such an outrageous act of treachery. Least ways that's what bookmaker and party Chairman Grant Shapps was told to tell the assembled party faithful. Shapps being a bit of barrow boy had to go one step further and call Mr Reckless a liar. According to Shapps "he lied and lied again" multiple lying, how utterly awful! Shapps probably was not the best person to talk about lying, given his past and the multiple identities, to wit, Michael Green and Sebastian Fox, that he once assumed to turn a penny for his Internet business.

Douglas Carswell had already jumped Dave's ship of fools, also defecting to the Loonies, and in an effort to save words, Dave aimed the same criticism at Mr Reckless "senseless and counter-productive" and "frustrating" but "but no loss". Well, Dave lost Clacton to UKIP, as Carswell easily took back his old seat.

Dave also lost civil society minister Brooks Newmark over newspaper revelations about his private life. Interesting to report that no bile was aimed at Newmark and also interesting to report that the man is a complete non-entity. Supposedly, he was minister for Civil Society - what does that mean? He only took on the job in July and now he has been replaced by Rob Wilson - we don't know who he is either. Let's face it, Minister for Civil Society is a non-job, all part of Dave's Big Society gimmick. Note, Shapps did not have anything to say about Brook's cross dressing behaviour, presumably conference has got used to ministers of state making a complete arse of themselves by sending explicit pictures of themselves to undercover reporters.

Although Dave was a bit upset with all this upset, he did find time to pre-release some of what's in store next time around for the nation - well mainly the younger part of it. He's going to lower the Benefit's Cap even further, from £26,000 to £23,000 and use the money saved to build 100,000 new homes, to provide under 40s the opportunity to get on the housing ladder at a discount. He also intends to toughen up the plight of young unemployed citizens. Those aged 18 to 21 would be given six months to find work or training - after which their jobseeker's allowance payments would be withdrawn unless they agreed to take part in "community projects" such as cleaning up local parks. Also this same group will struggle to leave home and claim housing benefit in the future. Still the nasty party then!

The impending Rochester and Strood by-election, November 2014, forced Dave to put the party machine at DEF-CON1, he told all his cabinet team that they must all visit the constituency 5 times each and everyone else should visit at least 3 times. If Mark Reckless were to retake his old seat faced with such determined opposition it might cause the Tory party to have a nervous breakdown.

Have some sympathy for the mortal citizen voters of this area, will they survive this onslaught from the fawning horde of MPs. Since it will not be just the Tories flooding the high streets and pubs, there'll be Greens and Loonies, Zombies and One Nation Labourites, all shaking hands and touting for selfies.

It would appear that UKIP have taken the high ground on the topic of immigration and Dave is determined to take that ground back. How you may wonder? Well, he intends to put an "emergency brake" on EU immigration. You may still be wondering how he is going to renegotiate one of the founding principles of the Single Market, the free movement of labour. He told Tory Conference, "Britain, I know you want this sorted so I will go to Brussels, I will not take no for an answer and when it comes to free movement - I will get what Britain needs."

For Dave's tough talk to be effective he really needs to do something before the next election, if he does not then UKIP will steal thousands of Tory votes on the immigration issue. The likelihood of reactive Dave actually achieving anything are slight to zero. Note: Net migration into the UK increased by more than 38% in 2013-14, that's 240,000 citizens, two-thirds from the EU. Dave told us he would reduce net migration to tens of thousands rather than hundreds of thousands in this parliament.

However, clearly Dave is prepared to go a long way to achieve his aims, in fact, all the way to the Australian parliament in Camberra. There he announced his new 'get tough on terror' strategy. Well, he's going to get tough, by taking away passports from people who want to go and fight for IS and, when they come back, he's going to tell them they can't come in and if he does decide to let some back in, they must be 'de-radicalised' and relocated. The number people who have left, the number of people that may have already come back, the number of people that may have been killed in action, and the number who may want to come back are all unknown quantities. The Home Office, the Border Force, Dave, no one has any real hard and fast figures. Currently, Dave is telling us that 500 may have gone.

An Unexpected Bill Arrives

Well, Dave popped over to Brussels for an EU summit, no doubt with an eye on finding some time to do a bit of renegotiating the Treaty of Rome, when Commission bailiffs gave him a bill for £1.7bn. This was apparently a top-up to Britain's budget contribution, required because the economy is doing so well. Dave went all red in the face and refused to pay by the due date, December 1st, 2014. Dave claimed he had been ambushed by the bailiffs and that he knew nothing about this bill. All very curious because the Treasury did know about the budget reassessment and we must infer that Boy George knew as well.

Within a few days Dave dispatched Boy George to sort the eurocrats out. George was triumphant, he halved the bill, he delayed payment, he changed the EU rules permanently. In reality, like a poor person in debt, George asked for time to pay, in instalments, and as for 'rule changes', no one else, who had been in the room with George, knew what he was talking about.

Back to Rochester and Strood

Dave's jubilation over George's brinkmanship was soon dampened by the election result from Rochester and Strood. Victory went to Mark Reckless and the Loonies, quite remarkable after Dave had 'thrown the kitchen sink' at this by-election. The best he could do was pledge to win the seat back at the general election. The Zombie candidate lost his deposit and came close to being bested by Hairy Knorm Davidson, from the Monster Raving Loony Party. Nick Clegg went into hiding.

Part 2: A Magical Land

A Disappointed Man acquires a vision

Even Tory stalwarts like Lord Tebbit, who described Dave's Big Society as a "logo in search of a brand" and original Tory-Boy William Hague couldn't find it within themselves to endorse Dave's vision. His key advisor and guru, Steve Hilton took flight to a teaching post in some US university - it was all too much for him, he rode off on his bike, mumbling something about Dave being 'reactive not transformative'. And we all know what a disappointment Andy Coulson was but few know how anti he was to Dave's Big Society.

For Baldricks like Hilton and Coulson, the Big Society was never meant to be the core of Tory thinking, it was a mistake, a misapprehension. The media heard the phrase "Big Society, not big government" and a mysterious conjurer's trick occurred, the Big Society took on a life of its own, people started asking what it was, what it meant. In truth, no one knew, it didn't mean anything; the fabrication factory was put on overtime. New Baldricks were recruited to breathe life into Dave's unintended vision, Red Tories appeared on the BBC's Newsnight with talk of communitarian socialism and the only game in town was becoming a social entrepreneur - nobody knew what they were either but they are doing very nicely creating something akin to a fictional Internet world like *Second Life*, where the only limits are your imagination.

A Magical Land sets out a key aspect of Tory thinking, patronage. Telling people what to eat, how much to drink, how much exercise to do through invasive schemes like Change For Life, an attempt to micro-manage citizens private lives. Charities and the so-called Third Sector have been co-opted via financial incentives to promote the government's approved messages. This is a smart move since the public still trust charities and therefore are more likely to listen to their apparent messages.

To reinforce its life-style messages the government has set up the Nudge Unit, based at No. 10. The work of the Nudge Unit is to use the mysteries of behavioural psychology, as originally developed by B F Skinner, and employ its insights into schemes that help people to live better lives - the same way that Skinner encouraged his rats to behave as he directed, by giving them an extra treat if they followed his directions.

If you doubt any of the above listen to Dave:

"We need to promote more responsible behaviour and encourage people to make the right choices about what they eat, drink and do in their leisure time." (David Cameron, foreword, A Healthier Nation, Policy Green Paper No.12, Conservative Party.)

Are you happy? Happiness is central to our leader Dave's Cunning Plans. If his blueprint for the Big Society is to become a reality, happy citizens are a necessary condition but happiness will not be enough to make this land a better place.

Dave has surveyed Britain's broken landscape, and quite frankly, he's disappointed.

The Tory government has your welfare at the centre of its schemes and this is underlined by its focus on happiness. Or perhaps we should say the quest for happiness. You may have missed this in the press but, you guessed it, the government have a whole army of people attempting to figure out if citizens are happy or not. At a deeper level they are attempting to figure how to measure the impact on happiness of economic policies. The ultimate goal is to devise a means of measuring wellbeing with the purpose of replacing growth as the key indicator of progress with one based on wellbeing.

For the current government, intervention in citizens lives is seen as a life-cycle strategy. This involves policing families through the early years via Sure Start centres and after, through the various school phases. And for those of you interested in the history of ideas, Sure Start is based like much else that politicians here do, on the US scheme called Head Start. Sure Start is another New Labour legacy item, one which our leader Dave says he is committed to.

Beyond intervention, patronage and guidance there must be something else, something to look forward to, some hope or else why would anyone strive. The answer coming from the Tory mind is a nation full of opportunities for strivers, where social mobility is assured. But Dave is also mindful that his people's security is vital, that's why he has you under surveillance 24/7, to protect you from the terrorists and yourselves.

The Big Society

Dave took a few people by surprise with his talk of a Big Society, in fact, apart from himself and a few visionary types that he keeps under the stairs at No. 10, very few knew what he was talking about - many still don't.

However, nothing in this world is genuinely new, most ideas are recycled, repackaged, or simply re-imagined. In the Sixties, US President Johnson kept inserting the phrase Great Society into his speeches, few knew what he was talking about either. Johnson never did clarify his message, he decided to napalm South-East Asia into oblivion instead and then there wasn't enough money available to build the Great Society.

Anyway, the Great Society didn't really fit with America's ruling elite's mantra: that taxation is theft, social justice is communism and those at the saturated fat end of the food-chain don't deserve to share in the Great Society.

Mr Cameron, or Dave, as he prefers his people to call him, is smarter than President Johnson. His Big Society doesn't appear to rely on massive spending by government, rather it relies on good will, charity, cooperation and self-help and, he also has plans to slim down larger people.

The creation of a Big Society is a part of the New Politics, state patronage started under New Labour and is now refined by the Tories (the Lib-Dems are of no consequence at the level of ideas). There are no new ideas at work here, the collection of ideas underpinning the New Politics are decades and centuries old.

Mrs Thatcher privatized our infrastructure and industry, now Dave's here to finish the job - by privatising every orifice of social life, yes, that does include the space between your ears. The Big Society is one, among many, cunning plans to control and privatise the social realm, all the bits that Mrs Thatcher never got to.

Be in no doubt, Dave's Big Society is no vacuous piece of hot air, to be dismissed as meaningless twaddle by Labour's yesterday men. Throughout the land the printing presses at Town Halls have churned out glossy brochures, complete with 'how-to' guides for citizens who want to work for nothing. The first 'schools' for Social Entrepreneurs signed up those with a passion for turning a penny from the free labour of others. The Hampshire School for Social Entrepreneurs led the way, offering a one year course, enabling people to set up businesses with a social purpose? Now, you have to admit it, this is a nifty idea, setting up businesses for society not personal gain... hope we haven't misunderstood the purpose.

Big Society: What does it all mean?

Well, that's like asking, what is the sound of one hand clapping. Central to your grasp of the Big Society idea, you need to imagine a morally heightened collective state of mental awareness, in which operatives choose to work for nothing in public service and survive on the succour and warmth derived from contributing to some mythical greater good. Well, this is the sort of ethos that Dave is trying to engender with his Big Society idea.

No. 10 says: the idea is "to create a climate that empowers local people and communities, building a big society that will 'take power away from politicians and give it to people'." This quote is a clarifying statement from No. 10 but there still appears to be some confusion in the land.

Critics say:

It is merely an attempt to hand state-financed services to the private sector and a cynical "cover" for spending cuts. Farming out services will cost the Government vast amounts and they will still act as the managing contractor, secondly, the Cuts would occur whether or not Mr Cameron got passionate about the Big Society. Apart from subsidizing co-ordinating sub-contrators, substantial costs will be incurred by training the first 500 organisers, £80,000 a piece over four years, plus the fee (unknown millions) to the training organisation, a so-called 'social action trust' called Locality.

The architects tell us:

The Big Society means injecting some oomph into communities, fuelled by citizens with a passion for volunteering. It means empowering citizens by engaging them in decision making at a local level. It means encouraging active citizenship, parish pump politics, i.e., citizen groups running post offices, libraries, transport services and shaping housing projects. It means giving people the right to veto council tax rises and for new providers to be able to set up so-called "free schools" in the state sector.

Ah, but, please don't start asking for 'local' flood defences, you see flood defence isn't a 'local' issue. This may be hard to take in as you watch your sofa floating down the high street, no, flood defences are a national issue, even if its happening in your locality on a regular basis. So while you're waiting for the walls to dry out, don't be idle, why not set up a free school.

Encouraging Vulture Capitalism

Opportunities to make money abound in the Big Society. Big Society Capital was launched with £600 million.

The Cabinet office tells us:

"Its mission is to grow a new market – social investment – and so make it easier for charities, social enterprises and community groups to access affordable finance. In turn, this will help them innovate, expand their services and develop better solutions to social problems."

The £600 million will come from dormant bank accounts, i.e. left untouched for over 15 years, and £200 million will come from the UK's four largest high street banks Barclays, Lloyds, HSBC and RBS. Can these banks really afford to go giving all this money away?

The Chairman of Big Society Capital is the one and only Sir Ronald Cohen, the genius behind 'social impact bonds', i.e.

rich people making money out of poor people (explained below). Can't you just see all those social entrepreneurs salivating over the prospect of tapping into this new pot of money.

Impetus Trust, the UK venture philanthropy association, has received a £310,000 investment from the Cabinet Office, designed no doubt to improve the private equity industry's public image, well done to them. Companies like these are into 'social impact investment'. These companies are not new to the Big Society tea party (in fact, they were not invited) just well placed to deal with the additional funds flowing from the tax payer.

Big Society Capital says its developing a strong, diverse and sustainable social investment market in the UK, enabling organisations tackling social issues to grow by encouraging investments made for social as well as financial return.

Social Impact Bonds

Monetizing schemes like social impact bonds can only be understood in the context of the Tory Cuts; £1.3bn from charities and up to 20% from the Sure Start interventions.

Sir Ronald Cohen, is busy launching a plan for rich people to invest in, for a return of up to 13%: the government will pay out rewards for future costs saved by social interventions. For years Cohen has developed social impact bonds, launched, as a way to monetise social problems and raise private revenue to solve them. It's a novel solution to extreme inequality, inviting the rich to make money out of the poor.

The first pilot began in 2010: bonds were sold to cover a charity's promise to reduce re-offending by 3,000 prisoners released from Peterborough prison. And how was this scheme to be evaluated? Well, badly, because it proved very difficult to track the saving where re-offending didn't occur; gauging improved health outcomes, saving to the justice system, social services, benefits, and police - not enough hours in the day to cull the necessary data.

A much bigger scheme

So being unable to properly evaluate the worth of a small pilot scheme, the ConDem's extended the idea of monetizing poor people to 120,000 problem families. This conjures up an hysterical scenario as some agent, (from a charity) working for a private equity cowboy, attempts to assess the needs of a schizophrenic mother, with six dysfunctional children and remedy her problems, and then, some chump from the local authority (the managing scheme agent) attempts to assess the success of this intervention. Payment will apparently be by results - but again, assessing the value of outcomes might prove a problem. This however will not stop the money go-round, as bonds will be sold based on the likely success of outcomes and the government will waste fortunes getting everything in place.

Why you may wonder does the government bother engaging the services of the likes of Sir Ronald Cohen. Does the government really need to attract private money for intervention schemes, which will undoubtedly lead to massive public losses. (Due to the fact that money will be paid out regardless of outcomes). The fact is the private sector cannot borrow money cheaper than the State, so involving private finance is just short-sighted; just think PFI schemes. And the irony is compounded by the fact that charities, denied funds by the government, will become proxy sub-contractors instead of the leading agents.

Privatising every orifice of social life

Dave's big idea then is to replace New Labour's Big Government with the Big Society, in which citizens, i.e. social activists transform the the coral reef of life, i.e. like fish do apparently.

Now, sit back and watch those social entrepreneurs scoop the pool. Thatcher privatised the infrastructure and industry, now Dave's here to finish the job - by privatising every orifice of social life.

The 'Big Society' is all about self-help and Samuel Smiles. Smiles told his readers, "God helps those who help themselves" and self-help is "the true source of national vigour and strength". In Sam's world, State help weakens individual effort and thereby weakens the whole of the big society. Add in a dose of Adam Smith's self regulating market efficiency to a meal of individual self-interested rational behaviour and there you have it: the recipe for the Big 'bang' Society.

The financial de-regulation of the 1980s was a precursor to Dave's Bigger Bang; total de-regulation of the whole of society.

Be in no doubt, Thatcher's Tory boys laid the historical groundwork for Dave's Bullingdon boys. The privatisation of Britain plc, begun under the Thatcher interregnum, will continue apace during the reign of Dave.

Thatcher put an end to ideas, put an end to the idea of struggle between owners and workers; she destroyed the industrial base of that struggle. The ships could be built in Taiwan, the coal dug in Mexico, the cars made in Japan and the steel in India. In services and utilities like transport and communications, gas, electricity and water could all be supplied by foreigners. Hard to wage a class struggle against a State that's divested itself of responsibility for producing and managing anything; except the behaviour of its citizens.

Dave does not have to worry about trades unions either, where they exist, they now barter for shells and trinkets like natives welcoming Captain Cook ashore.

So it's full steam ahead Captain Dave, sleeves rolled up and ready for action. Free up the markets, trust the markets. Let the food industry force feed children with its filthy muck, cunningly disguised in nice wrappers, unregulated. Where no natural market exists, create a market; make GPs accountants, remove oversight, make hospitals hustle for business, turn patients into consumers. And if the local school roof is leaking, let the parents put their hands in their pockets, there'll find a wide range of buckets at Dave's DIY World.

Reflections

A tea party took place in May 2010 at Dave's place to launch the Big Society, two years later, the 16 social entrepreneurs present reflected, all were clear on one thing, Dave's cuts made a mockery of the project and, although these people were generally optimistic, they were also clearly disappointed with progress. (Guardian, 7th May, 2012)

Hilariously, Dave and his Baldricks failed to notice that the Big Society is inclined towards socialism, with its intention to devolve power from the centre towards the locality, with cooperative development as its central driving principle. However, such inclinations were done for by Dave's cuts to local services. Further, the Localism Act 2012 set about demolishing all vestiges of community, with the introduction of the 'bedroom tax'. So, apologies to all those aspiring social entrepreneurs out there, Dave's Big Society has already been doomed by his own policies.

The Third Sector: Who's rattling the charity tin?

Few trust politicians anymore but they may trust a house-hold charity name like Age UK or Oxfam, or any one of the 160,000 plus charities operating across the UK.

A 2010 survey found that 75 per cent of the public believes that most charities are 'trustworthy and act in the public interest'. A different survey conducted a year earlier found that only 44 per cent trusted civil servants and just 13 per cent trusted politicians.

Charities, voluntary groups, and NGOs are, in the parlance of our times, referred to as the Third Sector, and the third sector employs more than 600,000 people. This sector plays a key part in government policy, firstly, as a key player in Mr Cameron's Big Society project and vitally, as propagandist for various government schemes.

"Charities perform a valuable role in campaigning for social change. The guidelines on campaigning should be revised to encourage charities to play this role to the fullest extent." (Cabinet Office Strategy Unit, 2002)

Since around 2000 the relationship between charities and the State has changed. By slow degrees the extent to which charities are able to promote an openly political message has loosened. To the extent that the present government is using charities to lobby for itself, i.e. the good causes, schemes and common sense that the State wishes to promote. Consider the case of the Remploy factory closures...

Charitable support for the Remploy closures

The government says that most Remploy factories are losing money and should be closed because the money saved would be better spent assisting the disabled and employers in the mainstream workplace - a lot cheaper.

Now, where we wonder do these ideas come from, yes, there is an idea embedded in there somewhere. Yes, the closures are about cuts but there's more to it. The idea is that disabled people would be better off in mainstream employment rather than segregated inside Remploy.

Back in June 2011, Liz Sayce, chief executive at the disability rights charity Radar, suggested 35,000 more people could be helped into work for the same cost as supporting the 2,300 Remploy employees. She was carrying out a review into disability employment, commissioned by the Coalition.

Reading Sayce's review, *'Getting in, staying in and getting on'*, it would be hard to argue against her ambition to improve employment opportunities for the disabled. However, it would be hard not to see her ambitions as starry-eyed, in circumstances of mass unemployment and intense competition in the low-wage jobs market. When the labour is shed from Remploy they'll wait a long time for their next job, if ever. The world beyond the Remploy gates has become more inhospitable, not less, in recent years.

(Note: When the government said it was going to close the Remploy factories, it didn't mean it was going to close the factories, don't be silly, what it meant was, it would be selling them off to the private sector and a paying a tidy subsidy for each employee retained.)

In the case of Radar we have a charity writing a State commissioned review of sheltered workplaces, which the State would like to be rid of and the review it has commissioned supports the notion that this would be good for all concerned.

State funding for charities

Over the past 15 years, the looser regulations surrounding charity lobbying has been accompanied by a very large increase in State funding for (some) charities.

Between 1997 and 2005, the combined income of Britain's charities nearly doubled, from £19.8 billion to £37.9 billion. By 2010, charities received more money from government than they did from voluntary donations. Parts of the voluntary sector had in effect become not for profit businesses. The old idea of self-sacrificing volunteers and jumble sales was becoming a thing of the past. Communications, raising awareness and education became the new core functions of many charities, in particular those receiving the bulk of their income from the State. For instance, The Child Poverty Action Group (CPAG) by the end of the New Labour period was receiving half a million pounds from State sources and only £76,000 from donations.

Charities come in all shapes and sizes and motivations. Most charities, 75%, received nothing from the State directly, and some well known charities like the RNLI have no truck with State funding, and some like Keep Britain Tidy or Citizen's Advice are largely dependent on State funding but are not into political lobbying.

The Government Lobbies Itself

Organisations like the Pedestrians Association, (PA) founded
in 1929, when cars were killing 6000 people a year, is of a
different type. Their good works included, pavements,
speedometers in cars, driving licences and speed limits. In
2001, the PA changed its name to Living Streets and receives
grants from the Department of Health, the Department of
Transport, the Scottish government and the National Lottery
which account for half of its income today. Beyond selling its
message, that it's better for children to walk to school, Living
Streets spends its time promoting its anti-car message. Clearly,
Living Streets is on message with government thinking.

Stonewall, the gay rights campaigning charity, have an even
longer list of State clients, including the Arts Council,
Department for Trade and Industry, Department of Health,
Home Office, Scottish government, Welsh Assembly, Greater
London Authority and the Equality and Human Rights
Commission. Most of these grants are restricted, typically for
'education', 'research' and 'health policy'.

Such charities are State funded pressure groups and their
ultimate aim is to influence public opinion. Naturally, you
might think, that's obvious, they are pursuing their causes but
what if their ability to do so becomes mainly reliant on State
funding. Do charities then become puppets of particular
ideologies? Guidance from the Charity Commission states
charities must only engage in political activity when it relates
to furthering the goals of the organisation.

"Political campaigning, or political activity, as defined in this guidance, must be undertaken by a charity only in the context of supporting the delivery of its charitable purposes. Unlike other forms of campaigning, it must not be the continuing and sole activity of the charity."

Under the 1968 Health Services and Public Health Act, the Department of Health (DH) was permitted to issue Section 64 grants to voluntary organisations for the provision of health services which would otherwise be offered by the NHS. Initially, these grants incorporated the use of hospices, centres for the disabled and family planning clinics. However, over time some kind of 'creep' occurred and groups were included to promote a range of public health goals, especially those involving eating, drinking and smoking,

The case of ASH, Action on Smoking and Health, is instructive. ASH was set up in the hope that it would raise £500.000 a year from donations, the money didn't appear, so ASH applied for and received a grant from the DH and by the 1990s, 90% of its funding was coming from the State. Alcohol Concern was set up with a £350,000 grant from the government. These organisations are part of a model of state-funded activism in contravention of the Charity Commission advice. The secure source of funding enabled these groups to become highly professional lobbyists, they had no popular mandate so they focused on networking, manoeuvering behind the scenes. Eventually, the government yielded to their demands, demands that they were not opposed to in the first place but yielding made it look like they were giving in to the popular will - which only goes to show that Dave didn't invent cunning. This was the government lobbying itself.

Civil Society

Until 2010 something called the Office for the Third Sector existed, this was rebranded under Dave as the Office for Civil Society. The Third Sector has been defined as "the place between State and private sector." Safe to assume then that it hasn't moved and that Civil Society is occupying the same space. Civil Society is the place where the will of the people is formed.

Interesting to note then, that the role of many so-called charities is promoting themes that the people are not exactly inspired by, if not hostile to; for instance, foreign aid, climate change, temperance, anti-smoking, 'sustainable development', radical feminism and support for the EU. You might suppose that the political elite, with their finger on the pulse of popular opinion through incessant polling and focus groups would sense the public's ambivalence to numerous issues and set policy accordingly but what we actually see is a kind of subversion of public opinion through the use of voluntary organisations, trumpeting phoney causes paid for by the same public that do not support these causes. For instance, the Department for International Development spends a fortune persuading the public that international aid is a good idea.

Rent Seeking

Under Dave's Big Society project, Civil Society is supposed to be the place where local people are making the choices but in that space the locals are being bombarded by messages from agencies sponsored by the State, about how they should live and what they should believe.

The man from the Couch Potato Council, Eric Pickles, banned local authorities from political lobbying, saying:

"Taxpayer-funded lobbying and propaganda on the rates weakens our democracy. So-called town hall newspapers are already closing down scrutiny from independent local papers. Now lobbyists are being used to sidestep transparency laws and shadowy figures are peddling more regulation and special favours."

Our thanks to the Secretary of State for Communities and Local Government for raising the topic of special favours because taxpayer funded lobbying by charities weakens democracy even more so, not just in terms of the true expression of popular will but also in terms of squandering resources. Those charities chosen to promote State messages are commanding resources that would otherwise be used to produce goods and services that consumers value, spending billions of pounds selling ideas is nonsensical. These agencies may be described as rent seekers, i.e. they do not create wealth, they tap into the wealth that exists and through the privilege of State endowments, they take command of the resources and prevent their use in more productive areas.

The word charity carries a halo effect, the term Civil Society conveys a notion of a private place out of reach of government and business. Charities operate within Civil Society, tapping into popular sentiment, addressing the excesses and disappointments of political and business decision making, campaigning for a better world. The halo effect and the perception of trust wears thin in circumstances where charities are no more than State sponsored message systems. And why wouldn't they be, over a three year period charities received over one billion pounds in public handouts, that is, money from government, the EU, the UN, and local authorities.

Charities and the end of the Big Society

Each year several thousand charities come and go, in 2011, 7,350 were removed from the register and 5590 signed on. Figures supplied by the Charities Commission show a similar picture of comings and goings in most years. However, the number of charities has declined in the past decade but not by a significant amount.

A big decline can seen following the credit crunch but we see gross income increasing. How much of this increase was due to government propaganda spending; we can only wonder. That's the beauty of living in an open society, it's full of wonder.

The press, specifically the Daily Mirror in this context, seemed to find the fact that over 7000 charities had disappeared cause for concern for Dave's Big Society. They thought that it signified a lack of willingness of people to support charitable good works, undermining the Big Society project.

"David Cameron's Big Society plans were ridiculed yesterday as it emerged more than 7,000 charities went under last year." The Mirror, (17/08/12)

The net fall in registered charities was 1,760, we don't know how many of these were one-off fund raisers that had run their course and no longer required; more to wonder about; reliance on partial surveys produce partial pictures. For instance, if a social enterprise, i.e. a business that performs a social purpose, e.g. helping prisoners on release, loses its funding due to local government cut backs, how can that be used as an example of the decline of charitable good works - as the Mirror claims. All such examples demonstrate is government reneging on its social responsibilities but then, that's the Tory project. The Big Society is about shifting responsibility and outsourcing the functions of local authorities. The Big Society project is as alive and well as Monty Python's Parrot but all those rattling the charity tins and clipping the coupons don't seem to mind.

The Politics of Happiness

What is happiness?

"It requires that basic needs are met, that individuals have a sense of purpose, that they feel able to achieve important personal goals and participate in society. It is enhanced by conditions that include supportive personal relationships, strong and inclusive communities, good health, financial and personal security, rewarding employment, and a healthy and attractive environment." Margaret Hodge

Wow, hold that thought! Hodge covers all the ground in what she says, she describes an ideal set of social circumstances. And the Dalai Lama tells us: "Happiness is not something ready made. It comes from your own actions". Something for Iain Duncan Smith to think about there?

The Happiness Quotient

If the Big Society is to succeed there is much work to be done, fundamentally people must become happier.

Apparently, our political elite are taking the idea of social happiness seriously. Work is in process attempting to measure the impact of policy measures designed to promote happiness rather than economic growth per se. Positive psychology has been used for years in the work place to encourage higher productivity but it's never been employed on a social scale.

The Office for National Statistics is to devise questions for a household survey, to be carried out up to four times a year, this began in Spring 2011.

According to Dave, the Royal millionaire, "there's more to life than money" and wellbeing is one of the "central political issues of our time". (Dave borrows most of his ideas, this one comes from Robert Kennedy.)

Other politicians, who think they know what Dave is talking about, say that it's not the Government's job to make people happy but they should take account of the policy effects on health and wellbeing. Indeed, almost 30 MPs signed a Commons motion, proposed by Lib-Dem Jo Swinson, arguing that "promoting happiness and well-being is a legitimate and important goal of government".

Beware! Psychologists at Work

A highly entertaining new report was published by Demos, with some help from PricewaterhouseCooper, entitled "Good Growth".

Demos, for those who don't know, is a Tory 'think tank' and PwC is the largest financial services company globally. The report we are told is tentative and preliminary, however, it's also important.

It's important because it's part of a futuristic trend in economics that attempts to reassess the role of government in the regulation of economic activity by identifying outcomes that enhance social wellbeing.

The focus of the report is "Good Growth", i.e. those variables that citizens consider central to promoting a happier existence than would be the case if the focus was simply on the growth of GDP.

Demos and PwC are not a bunch of happy clappers seeking to enlist citizens in a chorus of chanting for the sake of harmony.

Their report fits with ongoing studies by the World Bank, the IMF, the Stiglitz Commission and the United Nations, as well as, our own ONS - busy compiling Dave's 'happiness index'.

Why, we need to ask, all this effort on what used to be called 'welfare economics' now, when that branch of the subject has largely been ignored by our politicians and the City spivs at the sambuca trough.

The whole of the capitalist enterprise can be summed up as follows, production damages people, government intervenes to alleviate the damage, over time material conditions improve but the damage takes on new forms, less obvious and more subtle, more psychological than physical.

The current prominence of the welfare agenda recognises that the pursuit of economic growth has had its day. The idea behind the current spate of studies into wellbeing is twofold; to inform the political elite's decision making in order to quiet the troubled minds of the citizenry, and to use the current economic crisis to reassess economic activity in order to promote human wellbeing rather than profit.

And can't you just hear Louis Armstrong singing 'And I think to myself, what a wonderful world'.

Economics has failed, so send in the psychologists. In particular, send in B F Skinner, guru of behaviourism. All these reports and studies, all the data gathering are designed to capture the ingredients that Skinner identified for creating the engineered society.

A cynical view

Could it be that compiling a 'happiness quotient' will only serve to make politicians feel better, dare we say happy?

The big idea underpinning all this measuring of happiness is that the exclusive focus on GDP, as a measure of national success, has ignored much and might have led to a less than optimum outcome for the economy.

This might be a good time to point out that welfare economics is not new, it's just that part of the economics textbook that politicians prefer to leave to the market. Where it naturally gets ignored or the problems get exported to West Africa or sold as carbon credits on the global exchanges.

Beware ideologues dressed as sheep

Are we now being expected to believe that politicians are going to start taking our happiness seriously, in the midst of an economic crisis.

Yes, is the answer, our political elite have no ideas except recourse to a fantasy world - where everything and anything is possible. In this magic place new crusades will be forged and ideologues like the economist Richard Layard (now Baron Layard of Highgate) will carry the banner of happiness.

The Baron told us in 2007, 'What we need is an educational revolution in which a central purpose of our schools becomes to help young people learn the secrets of the happy life and the happy society'.

The Baron is of course standing on the shoulders of the great ideologue of the happiness movement, positive psychologist Martin Seligman. However, close up, Seligman is more behaviourist than humanist and Layard is more a moralist than economist.

These people are not leading us in a pursuit of happiness, they are redefining happiness; this is a moral crusade, this is social engineering and the factories are the schools.

Read Layard's *Happiness and the teaching of values* and make up your own mind.

Happiness is not a new idea...

Tony Blair's Strategy Unit was exploring the potential for promoting 'happiness policies' at a 'life satisfaction seminar' in Whitehall 2002. Defra was set to work compiling a 'happiness index', we don't know what happened to it or Defra. We think that Defra went into hiding following a toxic leak from a secret research establishment in Surrey, and this made them very unhappy.

Soviet dictator, Joseph Stalin, affectionately referred to himself as the 'constructor of happiness', he also took a great interest in imaginatively inventing statistics to prove it. Pictures of smiling Soviet peasants attending to their chores provided everyday proof; only Enver Hoxha's Albania provided more proof, i.e. through the great leaders published writing. Given that Enver was the only writer published during the period between 1944-1985 in Albania, we'll have to take his word for it. These men were real social engineers, although they did not score very high on the happiness index.

Happiness: update

Action on Happiness, launched Tuesday 12th April, 2011, boasts more than 9,000 members from 68 countries, all of them committed to building happiness. Well, actually, that's just the number of people who have signed up via the Action for Happiness website.

Happiness guru, Lord Richard Layard says:

"This is a movement for radical cultural change which can provide the basis for a better culture in the 21st century, we want millions of people around the world to form Action for Happiness groups to do just that - using the tools which we are able to provide."

Tools, tools, they've got tools....

Layard believes people can take specific actions to boost happiness. He acknowledges that genes and circumstances - factors outside one's control - will affect happiness. But he says happiness also depends on conscious choices and conscious reaction to what happens to us.

"Happiness is also contagious, so when we feel good we help

make others around us happier too," the website says. The website also provides visitors with a list of 'tools' which are not tools at all but rather a list of things to do, to guide you to the happy garden of life.

You can also download some free posters for your bedroom wall to make you happier. However, often the massive thrust of initiatives like producing a web site (with tools) do not always produce the desired result, sometimes a bit more is needed to guide people along your chosen path, sometimes people need a nudge; Dave has a plan for that too.

The Technical Bit: Measuring National Happiness

The plan is to measure both subjective and objective data, and in terms of the latter, try to assess the way our changing economic fortunes affect outlook. The Office of National Statistics (ONS) will be in charge of the data gathering. They will use the Integrated Household Survey (IHS), which will collect responses from 200,000 people - that's the subjective part of the study. The objective part of the study will rely on more traditional economic measures like GDP.

However the first results, published in 2012 were not conclusive in any sense. Importantly, some working on similar projects, across Europe and US, question the value of including measures like GDP. And economist Simon Kuznets, who first developed the measure in 1934, was adamant it should not be used to measure the wellbeing of a nation.

The essence of the problem in a nutshell is this: how do you add apples and pears and then agree with 30 other nations on your method, so that you can discover whether you are happier than the French? Dave will not be happy if he finds out our chums across the Channel are happier than we are. The Happiness Index is costing £2m a year.

Someone responding to a BBC questionnaire wrote: "Lord save us from mirth monitors, community grin assessments, and personal smile quotas."

How long will it be before Call Me Dave's Big Society commissars issue us all with Smiley Face stamp books? They say that in some US states utility bills are sent out with smiley faces on by way of congratulating consumers for cutting their energy consumption.

When Push Comes to Nudge

Nudge Theory: it's all part of a cunning Baldrick type plan to persuade you to live more healthily, on the grounds that healthy people are happier and will make a more positive contribution to the Big Society.

The Agenda

'Today we can't escape the fact that many of our most severe health problems are caused, in part, by the wrong personal choices. Obesity, binge-drinking, smoking and drug addiction are putting millions of lives at risk and costing our health services billions a year. So getting to grips with them requires an altogether different approach to the one we have seen before. We need to promote more responsible behaviour and encourage people to make the right choices about what they eat, drink and do in their leisure time.' (David Cameron, foreword, A Healthier Nation, Policy Green Paper No.12, Conservative Party.)

Here we see Dave taking time out in his busy life, i.e. dining with his chums up in Chipping Norton, to consider how we spend our leisure time.

Behavioural Insights Abound

This outrage has been designed by Cameron's Behavioural Insight Team, otherwise known as the Nudge Unit. That is a group of people being paid to think up ways to persuade us "to make better choices for ourselves".

The inspiration behind the Unit, which is central to Dave's Big Society plans, is behavioural economics expert Dr David Halpern. The Unit's focus is on all the problems associated with unhealthy life-styles.

Halpern is no stranger to the Cabinet Office, he was one of Blair's glove puppets under the last regime. His most famous contribution at that time towards a Nudge Theory was the paper *'Personal Responsibility and Behaviour Change'*. However, more recently, a 2008 book called *Nudge: Improving Decisions About Health, Wealth and Happiness*, by Richard Thaler and Cass Sunstein sets out the full picture. (P.S.

Sunstein works for Obama and Thaler works in the Nudge Unit).

The book explores "libertarian paternalism", or how public and private organisations can help people make better choices through market incentives.

In practice this will mean giving poor people food vouchers that can only be used on healthy choices. In New York, this thinking inspired Mayor Bloomberg to try to stop poor people spending their welfare vouchers on soda pop.

It get's worse.....

Halpern said in his blog that his work will build on the Mindspace report commissioned by the previous government. Mindspace looked at ways of changing people's behaviour by influencing not just what they consciously think but also by influencing their "automatic processes" – cues from the subconscious, from the behaviour of people around them, and from emotional associations that affect their decisions.

For year's we have grown used to advertisers' tricks, now the Government will be doing it as well. Even the Department of Health has set up a 'Behaviour Change Unit', informed by ad-men.

George Osborne told us in 2008:

"Our work with the world's leading behavioural economists and social psychologists is yet more proof that the

Conservative party is now the party of ideas in British politics."

People are, apparently, powerfully influenced by the people around them, this insight is one of the driving forces behind Nudge Theory for policy makers. The basic idea for policy makers is simple, tell people what the norms are and people will fall into line with those norms. Evidence from America suggests that a simple metaphorical pat on the back, like a smiley face on your energy bill, does the trick.

Beware! Behavioural Psychologists at Work

The Royal Society of Arts' Social Brain Project, which is spawning many of these ideas, says 'people are often systematically irrational'. And why would you care what irrational people think, unless you were engaged in a project to make them think rationally, you know, like you do.

When Orwell told us in his *1984* that "freedom is slavery" he must have had Nudge Theory in mind "We create human nature. Men are infinitely malleable." Big Brother wanted citizens to believe that 'freedom is slavery', this was 'doublethink at work'. Osborne is talking about creating a politics of behaviour, just another variant of doublethink. When Osborne talked about the Tories being the party of ideas, he should have said 'old' ideas.

Readers are reminded that in the 2005 election campaign the Tory slogans was 'Are you thinking what we're thinking?' If you weren't then, you will be soon.

Nudge theory is Skinnerism designed to reduce our comprehension and responses to a matter of unconsciously responding to stimuli, the focus is on wrong choices, the context in which behaviour can be understood and corrected.

New York is currently the lab in which much of Nudge Theory is being tested, where the politicians are 'changing the entire cultural landscape in order to make bad choices harder and good ones easier' to 'an overhaul of human behaviour' it's 'a vast population experiment with no control group'.

Dr Thomas A Farley, the main architect in New York's experiment tells us 'if we really want to change how we behave, we must change the environment in which we live'. Read Skinner's *Beyond Freedom and Dignity* (1971), he says exactly the same thing? It has taken several decades for Skinner's ideas to find favour, now they have.

Beyond Nudging: Refusing, sorry, Rationing Healthcare

People who over-indulge like smokers, drinkers and food gorgers can be difficult to nudge, the solution for such types is to ration the help they get. Hippocrates wasn't available for comment but 57% of doctors responding to a questionnaire (on Doctors.net.uk) said that they supported the idea of restricting and withholding healthcare to people who insist on pursuing their unhealthy lifestyles. So, because these recidivists will not desist they will be blackmailed by their medics. They will refuse non-emergency treatment to patients unless they lose weight or stop smoking, or at the minimum participate in nudge courses. A question mark has been placed over those who play sport and hurt themselves.

In March, 2012, the medical magazine, Pulse, published the results of 91 freedom-of-information (FOI) requests to primary-care trusts. Twenty-five of the trusts had some kind of lifestyle or bodyweight restrictions in place. So it seems as if there's an institutional twist to the prejudices of the medics - which is gathering pace as Dave forges on with his plans to make everyone healthier.

Dealing with drug and alcohol addiction

The thing about alcoholics and drug addicts is that they don't much care what you say and do; they care about where the next drink or fix is coming from. No one doubts the immense tragedy that addiction inflicts both at a personal and social level but these problems are not new. And Dave's latest scheme, to remove benefits from addicts to force them into work, is hardly likely to dent the problem.

The new universal credit will be used to switch the support that is currently on offer from 'passive' to 'active' intervention. Active appears to mean that the addicts will deal with their problems or lose their benefits.

The Department for Work and Pensions tells us that 160,000 dependent drinkers are in receipt of one or more of the main welfare handouts, 13,300 have been claiming for a decade. Almost 40,000 people who claim incapacity benefits have alcoholism as their primary diagnosis. Around 80 per cent of

Britain's estimated 400,000 'problem' drug users are also claiming.

Sir Ian Gilmore, Royal College of Physicians, special adviser on alcohol, said: "Current treatment facilities for addicts in this country, particularly those with alcohol dependence, are woefully inadequate....." And the man from Alcohol Concern said "At the moment only one in 16 people with an alcohol problem is receiving specialist alcohol treatment. In order to make this work, jobcentre staff will need to be properly trained in order to recognise when someone has an alcohol problem and to be able to offer the right advice." And the charity Release reminds us that this too was a New Labour reform, one which they dropped.

Each year, there are one million alcohol-related violent crimes and 1.2million alcohol-related hospital admissions. And you can expect the numbers to increase as addicts adopt plan B, more crime and violence.

Bread Crumbs

Every time you go shopping for points at your chosen supermarket you leave a trail of consuming behaviour. Now, Dave is backing the idea that his Nudge people tap into your shopping habits, using the information that your Sainsbury's Nectar card or Tesco Club Card contains. They'll be on the look out for too much fatty food and alcohol in particular. Now, you may be wondering how, having discovered that you are making poor choices, the Nudge Unit are going to sanction you. In truth, they don't actually know how but if points start disappearing from your card's tally, it could be retribution from those puritan nudgers.

From excess to responsibility: Dave's Plans for drinkers

A minimum price of 50p to "turn the tide" against binge drinking was put forward. North of the border, the Scots imposed a minimum price of 50p and booze cruises to Newcastle are the expected outcome. The ConDem's are also proposing a crack down on multi-buy offers, restricting opening hours and density of licensed premises, and sobriety schemes.

Dave was a trifle over-optimistic about the outcome of his new scheme:

"We're consulting on the actual price, but if it is 40p that could mean 50,000 fewer crimes each year and 900 fewer alcohol related deaths per year by the end of the decade."

Dave didn't discuss the 50p option, similar to the level agreed in Scotland, which would seriously damage alcohol sales and therefore slash the £9bn plus in annual tax revenues from sales of wines, beer and spirits.

The man from Wine and Spirit Trade Association, said:

"Minimum unit pricing will unfairly punish millions of consumers and businesses in the UK, while doing nothing to tackle the root causes of alcohol misuse."

And the man from Diageo said:

"Our position has always been that we don't believe there's a relationship between price and alcohol harm, so we're fully against minimum pricing," that was Mark Baird, corporate social responsibility manager for Diageo UK - maker of Guinness, Johnnie Walker, and Smirnoff.

Molson Coors, the US-Canadian brewing giant which makes Carling in the UK, also has a head of corporate responsibility and he says:

"Extremely cheap alcohol prices are not good for society and we believe some form of pricing intervention may be required."

He advocates no "below cost" selling, defined as below duty, VAT and a "nominal" cost of production for the brewer or distiller. The nominal production cost for each category of beer, wine, spirits and cider could be decided by industry bodies. All very interesting but it also appears like some form of industry appeasement. No matter, Dave finally decided that it was all too difficult tangling with the drinks industry and supermarkets - best to focus on the drinkers.

Spot the difference

Diageo Man says no to minimum pricing but the response from Coors Man seems much more measured, with his talk of below cost selling. Were they talking about the same thing in different terms or were they talking about two different things - who knows? We do know that Dave forgot all about the idea of minimum pricing in July 2013 and dropped it as the answer to the nation's drinking problems.

Curiously, in February 2014 he popped up with a new policy on drink pricing, no "below cost" selling.

Alcohol Concern said: "The idea that banning below cost sales will help tackle our problem with alcohol is laughable. It's confusing and close to impossible to implement and it will only affect about 1% of sales."

Meanwhile, Scotland's minimum pricing campaign hit the buffers due to legal challenges from the drinks industry.

Police Reform and Social Responsibility Bill, Dec. 2010

This Bill contained measures to reshape Labour's Cafe Culture approach to 24 hour drinking. Majorly, councils were given the power to impose a late night levy of £4,500 on pubs and clubs that cause public order problems. Also, councils will be able to prevent 'problem' pubs from staying open late. GPs and NHS trusts and members of the public will be given a key say in licensing applications. Fines for selling alcohol to those who are under age were doubled to £20,000.

24 hour drinking

A Select Health Committee report, (Jan 2010), on alcohol accused the Department of Culture, Media and Sport (DCMS) of "extraordinary naivety" over the introduction of 24-hour drinking. Their report was particularly critical of the DCMS, which sponsored the Licensing Act 2003 that allowed licensed premises to open around the clock from late 2005, and its claim that extended licensing hours would lead to more laid back, European-style drinking patterns in the UK.

"The department has shown extraordinary naivety in believing that the Licensing Act 2003 would bring about a civilised cafe culture."

Interesting that the Dept. for Culture didn't have a grasp of English culture.

Drug Dependency

Britain is winning the war against heroin and crack cocaine with a 10 per cent fall in users over five years, the head of the National Treatment Agency for Substance Misuse (NTA) told the world in March 2013. Chief executive Paul Hayes,, said among under 35's the numbers were "not falling, but plummeting" thanks to a "world class drug treatment system". (The NTA was merged into Public Health England in April, 2013.)

This is odd when we consider that that font of all knowledge, Nick Clegg, said a few months earlier that Britain was "losing the war against drugs on an industrial scale."

The number of registered addicts was down below 300,000, the number injecting drugs was below 100,000 and treatment programmes had cut offending rates, preventing almost 5 million crimes. The success story is due to a "world class drug treatment system". However, this system relies on funding from local authorities and can we expect them to continue their commitment in this age austerity?

A spokesman for Drugscope thought these figures evidence that the heroin epidemic of the 1980s was over but conceded the increasing use of new club drugs such as ketamine, GBL and mephedrone was a major cause for concern. We think that's what you call an understatement.

A Design for Healthy Living

Change 4 Life - you know it makes sense?

'Change4Life' is all part of a campaign, started under New Labour a few years ago and continued by the ConDems, to persuade citizens to eat properly. It is all part of a bigger campaign to encourage a state-approved healthy lifestyle.

Visit the Change4Life website and this is how you will be greeted....

"Well done! Visiting this site is your first step in making a Change4Life, and you're not alone."

Well Done! A nice big dollop of patronage there and the piece at the end about you not being alone is designed by the Baldricks in the Nudge Unit to provide you with a warm glow of being part of a much wider movement for change.

The message continues...

"The way we live nowadays means a lot of us, including our kids, have fallen into unhelpful habits. This means all of us need to make small changes to eat well, move more, and live longer."

Suffice it to say, the three sentences taken from the Change4Life website tell you all you need to know about the State's intentions in relation to its citizens.

Straightforwardly, citizens can't be trusted to eat properly, they've become unhealthy and have fallen into unhelpful habits; now they need help to get back to the correct path again.

We have been told for some time now that eating five portions of fruit and vegetables is supposed to guarantee a healthy lifestyle. Recently, a new study suggests that we should all be eating '8 a day'. What the commissars of health forget to mention is that there is no evidence that sticking to 5 or 8 portions a day does any good at all.

Five Scottish brothers, average age 85 years, have rejected vegetables all their lives and lived to tell the tale. The Artic Inuit and Kenyan Masai do not consume five vegetables a year, let alone a day and they manage to thrive, curious that. Let's hope these people never discover the Change4Life website.

Health secretary, Alan Johnson, back in October 2007, commenting on the launch of a report by the UK government's Foresight project said:

'We cannot afford not to act on obesity. For the first time we are clear about the magnitude of the problem. We are facing a potential crisis on the scale of climate change and it is in everybody's interest to turn things round. We will succeed only if the problem is recognised, owned and addressed at every level in every part of society.'

The report declared:

'By 2050, Foresight modelling indicates that 60 per cent of adult men, 50 per cent of adult women and about 25 per cent of all children under 16 could be obese. Obesity increases the risk of a range of chronic diseases, particularly type-2 diabetes, stroke and coronary heart disease and also cancer and arthritis. The financial impact to society attributable to obesity, at current prices, is estimated to become an additional £45.5 billion per year by 2050 with a seven-fold increase in NHS [National Health Service] costs alone.'

All very worrying then, half of the UK population will be like beached whales, marooned on their sofas, half dead couch potatoes in 40 years from now. Clearly, based on this evidence we must act. But wait, this is not evidence, this is a projection from a computer model. And the report definitely has not factored in the important contribution that will be made to healthy living by the mass consumption of games consoles like the Wii and Xbox Kinect. True these house-bound Olympians might suffer from vitamin D deficiency but they can take tablets for that.

The Health Survey for England tells us that obesity across all sections of the population has been falling for the past few years, so why the panic? Could it be that the State, having been spooked by zealots in the health business, now feel obliged to tilt at large fat windbags even though it doesn't make much sense. And another thing, why do Fish Fingers have added Omega 3, if there's any evidence of fish in those fingers it shouldn't be necessary.

A Tax on Fat - apply salt liberally

Where subtle 'nudging' fails it has been suggested by some spook elements that taxes might be applied. Ah, now what you need is a rigorous argument, backed by good research, that applying tax to fatty foods will achieve some stated aim, e.g. reduce ill-health associated with fat ladened food.

Enter the Journal of Epidemiology and Community Health (2007, 61, 689-694) who reported that various studies into cardiovascular disease in the past have concluded that an optimum application of VAT on fatty foodstuffs could avert 'up to 3,200 cardiovascular deaths' per year.

You can take that rather impressive claim with a pinch of salt due to the large numbers of citizens who succumb to cardiovascular disease. In percentage terms 3,200 is 1.7 percent of all deaths caused by heart disease - rather less impressive.

More seriously, those in Government and the media, who have a vested interest in blowing up headline information, do not always worry about the fine details of the research that will not persuade or sell.

Healthy lives, healthy people (White Paper Nov. 2010)

The White Paper told us that government intervention will be based 'on a rigorous assessment of the evidence'. Good, that's reassuring, given that we live in contradictory times.

'People in England are healthier and are living longer than ever' and "life expectancy is expected to continue to rise for both men and women' but we are also told about the big concern over the nation's unhealthy habits. For instance, there's the concern about people who consume too much fat, people who drink to excess, people who don't exercise and so on. However, put the worry to one side, the vast majority of citizens are moderate in their behaviour in all regards; it's just the way people are. And interestingly, moderate drinking, for instance, is associated with the lowest mortality rates in alcohol studies. There is evidence that tee-totallers will depart the planet before the drinkers do (evidence from the journal Alcoholism).

Unfortunately, the White Paper is not based on a rigorous assessment of the evidence, it also contains a fair few unsupported assumptions about health.

For example, regular physical activity keeps you healthy or gets you healthy. Recently, a TV programme told the story of a super fit fell runner who found it impossible to reduce his cholesterol below 7, by conventional wisdom he should have died long before now. Why isn't the man dead, no one knows, he's a statistical anomaly. But no one has proved a causal link between an active lifestyle and improved health. It might just be the case that you just feel better following physical activity, due to the release of chemicals in the brain; you might not be fitter at all, you might just think you are.

Also, doctors reading this might like to recall that over the past few decades acceptable measures of cholesterol have fallen. Once a reading of 7 would not have been considered significant, now 4 is becoming the recommended norm, soon it will not be too much cholesterol that's killing people, it will be too little.

The White Paper proposes an expansion of the Change4Life programme, this proposal takes no account of evidence that doesn't support the use of community wide behaviour control experiments. Beyond beating up poor people with vouchers, Change4Life is unlikely to impinge on the lives of the moderate majority.

Central to the White Paper is the notion that eating 5 a day is crucial to securing improved health outcomes but no clinical link has been established. Indeed, the Women's Health Initiative Dietary Modification Trial, found no statistically significant differences in the risk of breast cancer, colon cancer, coronary heart disease (CHD), stroke, or cardiovascular disease (CVD) between the intervention and control groups.

Obese people, the Paper assumes, are more at risk of premature death. A seminal study reported no relationship between overweight and excess mortality for cardiovascular disease or coronary heart disease (Flegal *et al*). Other studies have found negligible differences in risk of death among people with body mass index (BMI) values from 20 to 35 (that is, from 'normal' right through to 'mildly obese').

And finally, most political sound bites, never leave out the expected savings to the health service from citizens choosing the healthy option. Unfortunately, it costs the health service more to care for healthy people, who live long lives, than it does to care for those requiring treatment due to supposed poor lifestyle choices.

Healthy lives, healthy people slots into the Health and Social Care Bill which it's hoped will bring 'Healthy lives...' into being (including the switch on of Public Health England from 2012). And be in no doubt, no aspect of public health will be left out of the remit: health visitors, mental health, tobacco control, the public health "responsibility deal" with industry, obesity, physical activity, social marketing, sexual health, teenage pregnancy, and pandemic flu – not forgetting health protection, emergency preparedness and response. Hopefully, this will also include earthquake training.

Something to chew on for 2014

In March, the Mail and the Telegraph told us that 1 in 30 will die before their time due to eating processed meat. Now, reading the funny papers you'd believe that the study this amazing fact came from was exclusively about the effects of processed meat. It wasn't, the study was broadly concerned with examining the life-styles of meat eaters. The bottom line to this story is not that eating processed meat will shorten your life but eating *cheap* processed meat will shorten your life - it's cheap for a reason, it's designed for poor people. So good journalism, rather than the churnalism we get from the Mail and Telegraph, would have reported that poor people are dying before their time due to the life-style choices that poverty forces upon them.

The press release that accompanied this study's results tells us:

"One of the difficulties in measuring the effect of eating meat on health is the confounding effect of lifestyle on health."

There you have it in a nutshell, without confounding factors the world would look just like the Mail and Telegraph thinks it looks.

And keep in mind what Marshall McLuhan told us 50 years ago... the medium is the message, the content is "like a juicy piece of meat carried by the burglar to distract the watch-dog of the mind". If you do nothing else for the rest of your life, focus on the confounding factors.

It's not fat people that are the problem, it's fat cats.

The issues surrounding eating, health, and State intervention in citizens lives is complicated. The Government is telling people that their eating habits are unhealthy, it further presumes to tell us that this disorderly eating is storing up big trouble for the future. It might just be that the Government is coming at the problem of obesity from the wrong direction, i.e. by focussing on fat people when it should be focussing on the fat cats who drive the food industry.

Most of the food sold to poor people is junk!, recycled, reconstituted, reclaimed and fucking revolting. The poor get served up the left-overs, after the prime cuts have been sent off to Waitrose. Add sugar to shit, place in a deep freeze for ten years and then put it on the supermarket shelf and call it fish fingers. The poor should eat the packaging, that has more nutritional benefit than the contents and they wouldn't get fat. Ah, but soon some eco-warrior will want to take the packaging away from the poor because its destroying the planet. Stop press: some clever people at US firm Monosol will soon be launching edible packaging - tell the eco-warriors to get lost!

The Ministry of this that and the other tinkers around with information supplied on the packets, E numbers, fat content, salt etc., and then congratulates itself for getting one over on the profit gorging food industry. It's as if they are saying, well, read the back of the packet, it tells you that the contents in that fish finger was once almost a fish - what more do you want? If the State was serious about improving citizens health, artificial trans-fats would be banned and the food industry would be told to stop putting wall paper paste in our food, stop using bulking agents, stop reconstituting meat and fish and stop modifying everything we eat!

In 2003, the Food Standards Agency issued new guidelines for butchers on the amount of connective tissue that could be classed as meat, for beef, lamb and pork, 25% was allowed - why wasn't it zero? Connective tissue is inedible garbage.

Citizens do not need more labelling information, what they need is a government prepared to police food production for the benefit of citizens, then everyone would be far healthier.

Sure Start

Dave is concerned about everyone's welfare, throughout the whole life-cycle and he has plans to ensure that children have a good start.

Sure Start is another New Labour legacy item , one which our leader Dave is committed to. Sure Start is all about early intervention. The idea being that if you can spot the problems and correct them early, you end up with a bunch of good citizens. And for those of you interested in the history of ideas, Sure Start is based like much else that politicians here do, on a US scheme called Head Start.

At a deeper level, the idea is that poor parents have a skills deficit when it comes to child rearing, this can be remedied by education - you see these schemes are not just aimed at 2 year olds. They represent the transfer of the social problem of child poverty – poor children – into an individual problem of poor parenting.

However, a three year study carried out by the Office for National Statistics (ONS) found that early intervention had little or no effect on outcomes. All very interesting, when you consider that Britain is spending £5bn each year on various types of early intervention. A study by Birkbeck University supported the ONS findings, and some gloomy academics completed the picture by adding evidence from the US, Canada and Australia.

If you delve down far enough, I'll bet you could find a report buried somewhere that says, 'for every £1 spent by LAs in the early years saves £8 further down the road. In fact, there is Department of Health research that suggests just that - it was a work of fiction.

Perversely, however, the Sure Start scheme proved a big success with middle class parents. The target audience, poor people, preferred to steer clear of State sponsored interventions. And although evaluation of these schemes has been negative, the Tory government is pushing ahead with them.

Initially, Sure Start funding was ring fenced but that has been removed and funding has been cut. The Day Care Trust says that 250 Sure Start centres will close due to the cuts. Mr Cameron says he's committed to early years intervention. Contradiction, what contradiction? The cuts to the Early Intervention Grant (EIG) to local authorities, around 10% in 2011/12 fits perfectly into the Tory philosophy of 'more for less through greater efficiencies'. In short, the problem belongs to the local authorities, should they fix the potholes or fund childcare?

Only 6% of EIG is spent on parenting support and the view on the ground is that it is inadequate to meet the intervention aims of Sure Start.

Confusion

Something very confusing was happening to the Sure Start scheme. The Labour party was claiming in November 2013 that there were 578 fewer Sure Start centres. The Tories said no, there were only 45 fewer centres. Interestingly, the Department of Education's own figures support the Labour assertion. But Liz Truss, education minister, said no, it's still only 45 fewer, apparently, the other 500 or so have been 'restructured', some have been merged and new ones have been opened. Perhaps someone should tell the Education department, so that they can keep their records up to date.

Something more confusing was happening to the finances for the Sure Start scheme. The Children's Services Grants morphed into the Early Intervention Grants, the latter was phased out to be replaced by the Business Rates Retention scheme. The argument for the latter scheme is that it will encourage local authorities to grow the local environment and thereby retain a larger proportion of the business rates, which may be used for early years intervention schemes. According to Tory thinking this is all far more flexible than ring fencing monies for the purpose - obviously, it also means that the money may get spent elsewhere.

It's what the Tories call 'localism', i.e. freeing government from making difficult spending decisions about policies that it claims to support.

The national picture for Sure Start is clear, due the cuts to local government, centres are being closed and for those that are hanging on, the number of services on offer and trained staff are being scaled down.

Social Mobility: A Homage to Hope

Stalin pronounced in 1934 that equality was now "a piece of petty bourgeois stupidity, worthy of a primitive sect of ascetics but not of socialists". Clearly Joe had given up on the idea of creating a Communist utopia in the Soviet Union. In fact, by the mid-30s he had created a caste system, in which citizens were graded like eggs. In that circumstance social mobility didn't exist; party members begat party members. The masses had no prospect of going anywhere, except to an early grave or the Gulag. Joe's excuse for giving up on the ideal of equality was that the revolution had more pressing business like meeting production targets, individual striving hindered national goals.

A Homage to Hope

In the Capitalist world, the fiction that all have the opportunity to rise to the top with some hard work, where social mobility is encouraged, is central to all political and philosophical discourse. All that talk of equality, fairness and justice, most necessary within a system reliant on social harmony for increasing profits, and the notion of hope, even more so. The concept of social mobility is a homage to hope.

What is Social Mobility?

One definition might be, the degree within society that an individual can move up the food chain, the movement from scrabbling around on all fours for the crumbs from the rich man's table to actually dining at the table.

However, social mobility isn't really about some metaphorical individual's progress, it's a key measure of social progress.

Listen to the present ConDem Government... (1)

"A fair society is an open society, one in which every individual is free to succeed. That is why improving social mobility is the principal goal of the Government's social policy. No one should be prevented from fulfilling their potential by the circumstances of their birth. What ought to count is how hard you work and the skills and talents you possess, not the school you went to or the jobs your parents did."

What ought to count is an honest admission of policy failure in a world where hard work, skill and talent guarantee only an outside chance of producing a free and open society.

Social Mobility: the facts of life in Britain today

Bright children from poorer families tend to fall back around the age 6 relative to more advantaged peers who have not performed as well. Once these poor children begin to decline, this persists throughout their school career and beyond.

Is there something special about private schools? Could it be something to do with the belief that attending a private school (and the ability to pay) guarantees success in the world beyond school? Or does it have something to do with all that social capital you build up just by being there. The fact is that top professional occupations are dominated by the privately educated, from vice-chancellors and journalists to MPs and high court judges.

Old School Ties

A group called Future First was awarded half a million pounds to pilot a scheme to encourage social networks in 500 State schools. The initiative encourages the use of databases and emailing, texting and social-networking websites to help schools keep in touch with ex-pupils. Schools can then contact alumni and recruit them as pupil mentors and invite them to give careers talks or even become donors and fundraisers. Future First will collate data that will help pupils at a school contact former pupils from that school who are now in the world of work, for advice or work experience.

Life as a zero sum game

International comparisons may give the lie to the right-wing nonsense that increasing equality decreases economic incentives. For such types, government meddling in social mobility interferes with the natural order of the game - which is all about winners and losers, life is a zero sum game. In the competition for scarce resources; for the best school places, the best jobs and the best houses not everyone can be successful. Indeed, in the current circumstance few will be successful - the game is not fair.

In another context, Gore Vidal, once observed: "It is not enough that you should succeed. Others must fail."

The National Equality Panel tells us: (2)

"Britain is an unequal country, more so than many other industrial countries and more so than a generation ago. This is manifest in many ways – most obviously in the gap between those who are well off and those who are less well off."

An earlier report from the Sutton Trust (3) showed a decline in social mobility, there was a increasing relationship between family income and educational attainment, children between 16 and 18 from better-off backgrounds disproportionately benefited. The conclusion is straightforward, family income and background is central to social mobility in Britain.

Ask Ed Miliband, at 15 he got work experience in Tony Benn's office at the Commons. He was born into North London Marxist 'aristocracy' and he had parents who could open doors for him. Or perhaps we might ask Julia Hobsbawm, daughter of Marxist academic Eric. Once she ran a PR business with Gordon Brown's wife (it went bust) now she has a new business, Editorial Intelligence. EI's purpose? to put opinion formers and commentators in touch with each other, for a membership fee of £4000. We can only guess whether all that 'getting in touch' might secure some advantage for members.

People like Ed and Julia provide good examples of how family connections can help personal mobility. Individual stories provide some interest but it's the bigger picture that's important. Research gathered by The Equality Trust provides that bigger picture: (5)

"Greater inequalities of outcome seem to make it easier for rich parents to pass on their advantages. While income differences have widened in Britain and the USA, social mobility has slowed. Bigger income differences may make it harder to achieve equality of opportunity because they increase social class differentiation and perhaps prejudice." (5) This comes from a book called the *Spirit Level* which came in for a good deal of abuse from right-wing think tanks like the Policy Exchange and the Institute for Economic Affairs. The conclusions drawn in the book are drawn using statistical correlations, the critics point out that the data has been cherry picked and doesn't support the overall conclusion that more equal societies are better for everyone. In fact, the critics argue, the opposite conclusion may be drawn:

"As countries become more equal, life gets more miserable" (7) - just ask the Russians.

Britain is a very unequal place

The Joseph Rowntree Foundation in its 'Anatomy of Economic Inequality in the UK' concluded: (2)

"Moving up a ladder is harder if its rungs are further apart, and those who start higher up fight harder to ensure their children do not slip down".

The current government has all the data, it knows all about Britain's embarrassing performance in terms of social mobility. It has drawn up an impressive blueprint detailing how it will address the problem. It intends to intervene at every stage in the life cycle to encourage and support the most disadvantaged in their struggle up the ladder.

So will the strategy work? Conveniently, you might have to wait a life cycle to find out.

Monitoring progress on social mobility

We are told: (1)

"We have set ambitious goals for social mobility. Achieving them requires robust mechanisms to underpin the commitments in this strategy. So we are taking steps to ensure: external scrutiny; a new set of leading indicators to help us track progress; and ministerial activity to ensure social mobility is and remains at the heart of our policy agenda."

Yes, that's right, the government has set up a new quango to oversee progress, the Social Mobility and Child Poverty Commission. No one would deny that such an important set of issues must be policed by an external body. However, the government has changed its mind before on the subject of external oversight.

Sustainability lost its commission, the Sustainable Development Commission in 2010, with the government arguing it was far too important to be left to external monitors and now, social mobility is deemed far too important to be left in-house with government departments (or mainstreamed as they call it in Whitehall).

Point: the government doesn't appear to have a coherent model for monitoring the implementation of its schemes.

Economic Inequality

There is no need to wait a life cycle to discover whether the government's social mobility strategy works, the strategy is flawed, according to the National Economics Foundation (nef): (4)

"Firstly because public spending cuts will hit the poorest the hardest.

Secondly, their approach does not tackle wealth inequalities, leaving the wealthy to convey their advantages to their children.

Thirdly, initiatives are not universal, meaning that the richest will still segregate spatially and/ or opt into private alternatives. This will protect and reproduce the existing hierarchies in education and the labour market."

Social mobility refers to people's ability to transcend the problems created by economic inequality, those problems are absolutely getting worse in the UK and relative international comparisons show that the UK is among the least equal of developed nations. (5)

Conclusion

Bottom Line: the high degree of economic inequality found in the UK has created an unfair society. The low level of social mobility in the UK is a function of that unfairness.

Combating unfairness calls for a re-evaluation of the way the value of a person's social contribution is recognised and rewarded. Fairness dictates that the financial rewards of labour should correspond to its social contribution.

Several thousand tax accountants spend their working life helping individuals and corporations avoid paying their full tax entitlement. The Tax Justice Network estimate the loss to the exchequer of £25bn annually.

Contrast the negative efforts of the tax accountant and his rewards, with those of a home carer, who saves the state a small fortune, providing a higher level of personal care than any hospital or care home, for a pittance. The reward here is negligible and the contribution hardly recognised by society. These are the contrasts that lay at the heart of the problem and they will not be tackled by *Opening Doors, Breaking Barriers* because the strategy is based on encouraging individuals to improve their circumstances.

Individual improvement is always to be applauded but the idea of a critical mass of individuals rising above their circumstances to generate an additional 4% of GDP by 2050, as the ConDem's do, is a homage to hope, unless, we have some policies to deal with economic inequality.

Some superficial arguments over inequality decry the idea of tackling it, saying as some pundits do, that 'we can't all be equal' because inequality is a natural state. It may be true that individuals can't all be the same but a strategy to combat inequality is not about making everyone the same, it's about making society fairer because there's nothing natural about an unfair society and that's what Britain is - according to the government's own account in *Opening Doors, Breaking Barriers: A Strategy for Social Mobility.*

Sources:

1. Opening Doors, Breaking Barriers: A Strategy for Social Mobility April 2011.

2. An anatomy of economic inequality in the UK: Report of the National Equality Panel, Jan. 2010

3. Intergenerational Mobility in Europe and North America., April 2005, Sutton Trust.

4. Why the Rich are Getting Richer, The determinants of economic inequality, NEF report

5. The Spirit Level, Wilkinson & Pickett, Penguin 2009.

6. A Bit Rich, NEF report.

7.   Beware False Prophets: Equality, the Good Society and The Spirit Level, Peter Saunders, Policy Exchange

Terror, Surveillance, Snooping and Cyberwar

Apparently, we are at war, with terrorists, criminals and drug barons and in order to protect us the government needs to listen to all our conversations, read all our emails and track our web use. You know it makes sense or does it? Well, Call Me Dave thinks it does, Theresa May thinks it does and so does that well known security expert Nick Clegg (he's now having second thoughts or rather he thought he needed a campaign to make himself look interesting).

Well, in truth, these people do not know if it makes sense or not - that's what they pay the spooks for and the spooks have told them it's all necessary - so it must be. And silly ex-Tory ministers will add fuel to their fire by saying silly things: "A majority of people will accept that an ideological battle means that the authorities will need greater powers to intercept the communications of extremists." That came from discredited defence secretary, Liam Fox responding to the alarm caused by returning ISIS fighters from the Iraq conflict. And we know that you will feel the warm glow of contentedness washing over you when you learn that the Met has 'shoot to kill' Cressida Dick on the case of the returning Jihadists. We can only advise returners to walk rather than run - Jean Charles de Menezes made that mistake because he was late for work. Note: Dec. 2014, Cressida Dick is standing down from tracking returning Jihadists. She has been headhunted by the Home Office to do, well we don't know what her role will be, the Home Office is not saying? Also, for the record, Dick has always denied giving the 'shoot to kill' order in the case of Jean Charles.

However, the plan is to install a mass surveillance system, which will put Britain on a par with China, Vietnam, Iran and Syria, and yes, the USA. And Britain is well placed to set up such a system since it is British companies that supply most of the technologies to all the nasty regimes around the world, who care nothing for their citizens civil liberties.

Internet service providers (ISPs) will be forced to install hardware that would give law enforcement real time, on-demand access to every internet user's IP address, email address books, when and to whom emails are sent and how frequently - as well as the same type of data for phone calls and text messages.

Also, not a few MPs and peers have urged the government to consider introducing censorship legislation that would force search engines to censor search results to block material that a court has found to be in breach of someone's privacy. They have in mind protecting wealthy individuals and companies who take out "super-injunctions". Several hundred requests have been received by Google to take down search results, under new 'right to be forgotten' legislation. Wikipedia has also been hit, a number articles, although still there, cannot be accessed via search engines.

The government is also keen to introduce the Online Safety Act, which would force ISPs to block access to pornography by default. Users would have to contact ISPs for access, having established some kind of age verification. Dave also wants websites playing music videos to install age verification systems, to stop children seeing grandmother Madonna prancing around with next to nothing on. They also considering how they can use ISPs to combat copyright infringement by blocking access to offending websites.

Recap: the ConDems are proposing legislation to protect children from porn and music videos, to protect footballers caught with their trousers down and to protect us all from nasty people.

What evidence is there that these new surveillance measures are necessary? How do independent experts assess the reliability of this evidence? Will the spooks provide any evidence or will they claim it's all too secret to be shared? How will we know if the proposed measures are protecting us effectively? And importantly, how much will all this cost, assuming that someone has bothered to cost it at all. These are just questions, don't expect any answers.

However, with the Communications Data Bill, Britain was attempting to get ahead of the pack, the Bill was announced in the Queen's 2012 Speech. The idea behind the Bill was to make it easier to discover who has contact with whom, when and where, via internet services such as Facebook, Gmail and Skype. ISPs would be expected to intercept and store the relevant data for 12 months. In the land of the free, the liberal democracies, can use the Act to eavesdrop on citizens, just in case they might become dissenters. The Bill appears to have hit the buffers and as of mid-2014 is still not passed into law. However, given the news over Prism and Dishfire we have to ask why the government needs to put a sham legal gloss on its snooping activities, especially when the cost of this legislation is put at £1.8bn.

The Internet provides a means to convey *samizdat*, to give a voice to the dissenters, to reach out in a way that radio and TV do not allow the average citizen to do. Any fool from GCHQ can eavesdrop on Facebook and Twitter but will struggle to do much more no matter how much money they throw at their snooping projects. Savvy web users would do well to use the web independently of Google, Facebook and Twitter, these money grubbers are the unwitting assistants of the State snoopers as they amass a vast store of personal data for their own marketing purposes. And let's not forget, Google's own snooping activities whilst gathering data for its Street View project. Google's software mistakenly gathered data from citizen's wi-fi connections as it filmed the streets. Well, that's what Google told the world, a US investigation found that the engineer who designed the software specifically intended to collect and analyse the data. (Big Brother Watch website) The company was fined $25,000.

Local Authority Snoopers

The Regulation of Investigatory Powers Act (RIPA) is another part of New Labour's legacy. The Act has wide-ranging surveillance powers introduced to tackle terrorism and serious crime but is being used regularly by councils to tackle relatively minor problems and to routinely snoop on citizens. Councils are using RIPA to snoop on residents leaving their bins out on the wrong day, on the look out for dog-foulers, people 'fly tipping' donations outside a charity shop, and covert surveillance on their own staff.

This Act is 'self-authoring' which means that councils can decide for themselves to use the legislation and they have and they do, hundreds of times a year, to little effect, prosecutions have been few. 372 local authorities in Britain have conducted RIPA surveillance operations in 8,575 cases over two years and managed only 300 convictions. Incredibly, some authorities said they didn't keep records of successful outcomes? (The Grim RIPA Report, BBW)

The cost to rate payers of this grossly irresponsible use of anti-terrorism legislation is impossible to calculate but Dave has had enough:

"We will ban the use of powers in the Regulation of Investigatory Powers Act (RIPA) by councils, unless they are signed off by a magistrate and required for stopping serious crime." (Cabinet Office)

Which should mean, when it happens, that councils can no longer use RIPA since they have no business dealing with serious crime - that's what the police and real spooks are for.

Voice Risk Analysis (VRA)

Many local authorities are keen on the use of 'voice risk analysis' to catch people trying to fiddle their council tax discounts. The idea here is akin to the use of lie detectors, where software is used to gauge how nervous people are when answering questions.

Campaign group False Economy gleaned information about the use of VRA from FoI requests of more than 200 local authorities.

The VRA software was originally sponsored by the New Labour government, to the tune of £1.5m but the coalition cancelled their support in 2010. The DWP decided that the software didn't work. Local authorities have continued to fund the use of VRA, having been convinced by outsourcing cowboys, Capita, that its use provides a valuable tool in the fight against benefit cheats.

However, language experts tell us:

"From the output it generates, this analysis is closer to astrology than science."

Councils seem to believe that whether it works or not is beyond the point since if people think they have got a high tech weapon in their armoury, they will be more honest in their claims for council tax discounts. There appears to be a fly in the ointment because it's not generally known that councils are using the weapon, so why would it encourage honesty?

Citizen Snoopers

"If you're worried, so are we, don't worry alone..."

Radio request for citizen spooks: The Met Police placed radio adverts asking citizens to be alert for odd behaviour. The ad' campaign seems reminiscent of War-time calls for vigilance, 'careless talk costs lives' and all that. As you would expect there's a dedicated call centre waiting for all that vital citizen intelligence to come pouring in - who needs M15?

See them, report them: a local council snooping scheme was launched in London and could eventually be rolled out across the country. Residents were being told: "We need your eyes and ears to help us wipe out enviro-crime." SNOOPING residents are being offered rewards of up to £500 to spy on their neighbours.

Let's look at that again....

"If you're worried, so are we, don't worry alone..."

If you are worried, you've got every right to worry because you are alone, when you ring the bell at your local police station and the voice speaking to you on the answer phone is coming from several miles away. Your police station has become a victim of Dave's Cuts!

Cyberwar - the new panic

The cost of cyber crime is estimated to be between £18bn and £27bn a year. And cyberwar is a reality and cyber espionage is perfectly logical and real. The Chinese have a cyber crack commando unit tasked with stealing secrets from commercial and military targets abroad but they are Dave's new best friends, so no worries for us but America are mightily concerned.

The National Audit Office warned that threats were evolving and that more cyber crime fighters were needed to meet these threats but education experts have warned that it could take 20 years to fix the skills gap.

In 2011, ministers announced funding of £650m to implement the UK's Cyber Security Strategy, which set out the risks of the UK's growing reliance on cyber space.

The strategy identified criminals, terrorists, foreign intelligence services, foreign militaries and politically motivated "hacktivists" as potential enemies who might choose to attack vulnerabilities in British cyber-defences.

New regional police cyber crime centres and a trebling of the size of the Police Central e-crime Unit has helped but there are not enough techies in the pipeline to meet the challenge.

The government's proposed Strategy promises to protect citizens' cyber freedom, so don't have nightmares.

Reference: *The UK Cyber Security Strategy 'Protecting and promoting the UK in a digital world'* (2011)

Prism and colourful ignorance

Watching from afar, i.e. a Russian airport, Edward Snowdon decided that he didn't want to face the same justice as Bradley Manning for revealing the private moments of the NSA. Snowdon's revelations were to some extent more far reaching than Manning's, involving the British government and the major Internet players like Google, Facebook and Microsoft.

The Empire of America is spying on the world of Internet communications using a snooping program called Prism. At an internal presentation, given to NSA employees, it was revealed that the program was used to access data held by the world's major Internet companies, including Facebook, Google, Microsoft, Apple, Yahoo and Skype. These companies all claim to know nothing of the program's use and are keen to assure citizens that they take your privacy seriously. All very mysterious, given that this has been going on for years and our own 'listening spooks' at GCHQ have been receiving reports from the NSA, acquired using the program. Further along, we discovered that the NSA were using a text message collection system called Dishfire; the big telecoms companies were shocked and surprised.

Politicians of all shades here also claim to know nothing about these programs and its use or GCHQ's involvement. Laughably, opposition MPs lined up to ask Theresa May, the Home Secretary, questions in the House - the odds of Ms May supplying a useful response were inestimable, according to William Hill, the bookmaker.

The interesting thing about Prism is that it is able to access the contents of emails and live chat. This takes it way beyond the now discarded Data Communications Bill, with its focus on capturing metadata, i.e. simply listing the destination and duration of communications.

News of the use of Prism came to light in June 2013 and the big Internet players were mightily embarrassed by it since it made it look like they were colluding with the spooks.

A few months later we saw Microsoft and Google preparing to sue the US government to win the right to reveal more information about official requests for user data. This heralded the start of a legal battle over the Foreign Intelligence Surveillance Act (Fisa), the mechanism used by the National Security Agency (NSA) and other US government agencies to gather data about foreign Internet users.

Conclusion

National security is usually given as the justification for spying on the citizenry. The mass surveillance that Edward Snowden revealed was undertaken to protect you against terrorism and crime.

According to Charles Farr, the government's top security official, social media chatter can be monitored because it is judged "external communications". Farr just wants you to know that no laws are being broken when the spooks are listening to your conversations. This is analogous to torturing someone in a foreign country and claiming we don't torture prisoners here.

And if the law is being broken when surveillance takes place, how would we know. Well, a number of agencies are tasked with watching the snoopers, like the Office of Surveillance Commissioners, there's a commissioner for intercepts, and one for the intelligence services - he's part-time but has a staff of one. There's also the investigatory powers tribunal taking care of complaints. That's all very reassuring, isn't it? Well actually no, all these commissioners are not part of some joined up oversight project, quite often they just trust that the snoopers are doing the right thing. A report from the Intelligence Services Commissioner tells us that only 17% of warrants for intercepts were checked by his office, there's only so much one man and his sidekick can do.

Bottom line: Oversight is weak, accountability is non-existent. So, citizens should take it on trust that the snoopers are acting in the public and national interest. It's a classic 'Catch 22' circumstance, the interests that inform the actions of the snoopers cannot be relaid to the public because its not in the public's interest to know. We hope that's clear! In the meantime, Ms May has another 'initiative' to assist in the fight against the terror threat, a leaflet campaign entitled "Run, Hide, Tell", which seems reminiscent of the US "Duck and Cover" campaign of the 1950s, designed to protect citizens following a nuclear explosion.

And did you Know?

In 2013, more than 570,000 data requests were made to companies by the police, security services, HMRC and various public bodies, including local councils and organisations like the Charity Commission, Environment Agency and Health and Safety Executive. Why these requests were made will forever remain a mystery.

Still, if you've got nothing to hide, you've got nothing to fear. Now, remind us again, why wont Dave release those Blair-Bush conversations for the Chilcott Inquiry?

Part 3: The Future of Welfare

Setting the agenda

A YouGov poll for the TUC in 2012 found that, on average, people think 41% of the welfare budget supports the unemployed – the true figure is 3% – and people believe the fraud rate is 27%, the true figure is less than 1%.

Now where are people getting all these ideas from, could it possibly be from ministers working out of the Department for Work and Pensions? Research carried out by the Guardian tells us that the word fraud was used in connection with benefits 85 times in government press releases during 2012. And in the same period, analysis of the media shows the term "benefit cheat" was used 442 times.

Examples:

1. The Daily Mail (April 2013) told us that murderer Mick Philpott was living on welfare benefits of £100,000 a year. In fact, Philpott was in receipt of £67,000. The Mail managed this trick by assuming he was a working tax payer.

The Mail's pitiful attempts to present Philpott as the tip of an underclass iceberg, representative of all that's wrong with the benefits culture, is statistically unsound. Philpott had seventeen children living under one roof, that's rare, if not unique, it's certainly not a typical example of a family living exclusively on State benefits.

2. In January 2012, The Mail found someone intelligent enough on its staff to make a Freedom of Information request. Now, this is odd behaviour for the Mail because their norm is making stories up, and so armed with the stat's they made things up. Their headline read:

"The 190 families with ten children who cost you more than £11million in benefits A YEAR"

What the headline does not reveal is that the £11m figure is only a potential figure, i.e. if these 190 families were to claim everything they were entitled to or eligible for then it would reach the Mail's mythical target figure. So these families were not costing you £11m a year.

3. The man responsible for the benefits cuts regime, Iain Duncan Smith, misrepresents the figures on welfare spending all day long. He told the Telegraph (March 2013) that under Labour, fraud and error in the tax credits system cost over £10 billion - the actual figure between 2003 and 2010 was £11.16bn. However, breaking down the figures, we see that only £1.27bn was deemed to be fraud, which leaves a lot of error to be explained by HMRC.

Duncan Smith then went on to claim that much of this fraud was perpetrated by foreigners taking advantage of our tax credit system. He said:

"It will come as no surprise therefore that fraudsters from around the world targeted this benefit for personal gain."

The fact is, he can't know that, because HMRC do not know the ethnicity of those claiming tax credits.

Beveridge: The Welfare State 70 years on

Work and Pensions Secretary Iain Duncan Smith said the soaring cost of the welfare system had lost touch with Beveridge's original vision of ensuring 'freedom from want'.

He told the world:

"Beveridge's pioneering vision for welfare has been completely lost. 'The system is complicated, expensive and open to abuse. Our reforms will restore confidence and bring the benefits system back to Beveridge's founding principles."

And to reassure us of his Tory credentials, he said:

"We will deliver his vision of a Welfare State that provides a safety net for those who need it, without stifling incentive, opportunity or responsibility."

This may sound like good old fashioned Daily Mail sense. We are being offered the proposition that Beveridge had a vision that got itself out of focus and crucially that that distortion of the original vision has led to a stifling of incentives and opportunity....

Interesting to relate that Beveridge himself told us:

The state "should not stifle incentive, opportunity, responsibility; in establishing a national minimum, it should leave room and encouragement for voluntary action by each individual to provide more than that minimum for himself and his family".

When we revisit Beveridge we see that the State had no choice about putting in place the safety net of social welfare support. The private sector was failing the economy prior to the war, the whole social fabric was in disrepair, housing, road, rail, coal mining, steel making, health service, etc., in particular health was in a chronic state. Private provision was chaotic and importantly could not deliver or begin to guarantee full employment, which was by then generally accepted as the wisdom of the day. If full employment was to be the aim, the State would need to take greater responsibility for the health of the nation and the management of the economy.

The Beveridge report may have identified five 'giant evils' in society: squalor, ignorance, want, idleness and disease but this should not be seen as the dawn of the New Jerusalem. Stamping out these evils was vital to building a modern economy. What followed from the Beveridge report was the minimum of social provision, nothing to encourage anyone to decide to turn benefits cheating into a life-style. In fact, so-called National Assistance was already in place but in the popular mind this was seen as 'poor relief', what Beveridge did was put forward the idea of something more rigorous and less tainted by social stigma, i.e. National Insurance based on compulsory contributions from workers and employers, so there was not much State largess at work here.

When Iain Duncan Smith talks about Beveridge's vision he's misunderstanding the moment, if he tries to see the minimum of social support suggested, outside of the context of the need to build an economy working close to the production possibility boundary and, at times of market failure, to have a backstop in place for idle workers.

A sense of entitlement

At what point in time the minimum provision suggested by Beveridge became the sense of entitlement to welfare handouts, that so concerns Duncan Smith, is difficult to pinpoint but the curse of the business cycle bears a large portion of the blame. The State management of the economy that took place in the post-war period was just as hit and miss as the free-for-all that reigned previously (and reigns now). Over decades following the war a reserve army of labour has been parked on benefits, rising and falling in size with the fortunes of the economy.

The growth of expectations

We need to take account of the growing importance of the growth of expectation among the workers, in terms of material wellbeing. The growth of those expectations was essential to the producers. The consumer society had come to pass, the distinction between wants and needs had become blurred. State 'handouts' that merely put a few scraps on the table, to tide workers over, were no longer sufficient to meet the wants of a new generation. Even given the huge growth in the economy over the past seven decades, the increase in the cost of the benefits system has been dramatic. In 1948 spending on benefits accounted for 10.4 per cent of Britain's total income, against 24.2 per cent in 2012. The difference between now and then, not withstanding population increase, is not just about expectations and consumption patterns, a key major difference is that now everyone is on benefits, from the poorest to the well off middle class and beyond.

However, the important point here is that it was not the displaced workers, the incapacitated or the homeless who drove up the welfare bill, it was the politicians. Successive governments increased and expanded welfare provision to suit their policies and to conceal their failures. The tens of thousands of ex-steel workers and coal miners placed on incapacity benefit by Thatcher to conceal the true unemployment figures cannot be redacted by Duncan Smith to suit his arguments now. Although Atos Healthcare are doing their best to get Thatcher's hardly incapable workers off of benefits. We should also remember that it was Thatcher's 'property owning democracy' which created the shortage of social housing, that enabled the private sector landlords to help themselves to the cash by driving up rents for those on benefits. Then, it was New Labour's inept managers who failed to anticipate the impact on the benefits payment system of

European enlargement, they could have put quotas on new comers from eastern Europe but failed to do so. The openness of Britain's borders, under New Labour, hastened the nation's descent into a low-skill-low-pay economy, where benefit top-ups became a necessity.

The proposition from Duncan Smith that Beveridge's original vision has been distorted is not true. In reality the vision got larger of necessity, responding to changing economic circumstances and political manoeuvring. Duncan Smith's proposition that he can restore Beveridge's vision back to its original limited ambition is nonsense.

It's not nonsense simply because it's impossible to turn back the clock, it's nonsense because Duncan Smith has already succeeded in mangling Beveridge's original vision, which was based on fairness, on a contributory system of support through National Insurance payments. Now, a displaced, dislodged worker has to wrestle with the benefits system to secure any financial support. Duncan Smith's benefits system is in no fear of stifling incentive, opportunity or responsibility; anyone who chooses to create a 'life-style' on benefits is living a very rare existence, that is, a life pretty much devoid of style.

Making adjustments

The present coalition government believe that changing attitudes is the way forward, that is, the attitudes of workers and potential workers, if only they could instill a more thrusting and dynamic activism by removing any temptation towards idleness, then we will be on the optimum path to success.

The fixation with idleness overlooks a far greater problem, the inefficiency of success.

The evolution of capitalism has not led to the survival of the fittest, that is, natural selection has not assisted those most able to adapt, it has led to malignant distortion by assisting those most able to manipulate the market. Pick a market, any market and then look at how the big players in every market conspire against the consumers. And in every market observe how smaller players feast like parasites on the left-overs that they call market opportunities. The seedy, underhand, conniving behaviour of the business world is not some closely guarded secret; insurance companies rob old people with their over-50s plans, banks fiddle global interest rates to conceal their own failure at a cost to everyone else, shops sell food falsely labelled. All rotten to the core, unable to provide a honest service.

Those who inhabit the so-called dependency culture are publicly ridiculed, those who inhabit the thieving enterprise culture are rewarded with knighthoods and lavish pensions. According to Adam Smith, unfettered markets would provide the optimum conditions for wealth creation. That optimum would be reached by the invisible hand of the price mechanism. Following Smith, a host of philosophers provided utilitarian underpinning to his economic theory. If all economic agents, buyers and sellers, maximised their personal utility without damaging the utility of others, then everyone would be better off - utopia? Smith's view of human nature was that it was self-interested but it was balanced by a sympathy for others - Bless his heart.

Adjusting expectations

The Tory agenda is not exclusively focused on ending an imagined dependency culture, its key focus is realigning the mentality of the middle income and low income majority.

Adjusting expectation, that's the new biggest game in town. In the public sector pay rises have been frozen, in the private sector they are going backwards, inflation erodes earnings further and low interest rates erode future pension incomes. In real terms, average incomes in 2013 were the same as they were in 2005.

The national debt must be brought under control and everyone's expectations must be adjusted to face up to this imperative. It's imperative because the 'markets' demand it and the 'markets' fund the debt. So we must convince the 'markets' that we are serious about reducing our long term debt obligations. This notion of appeasing markets is pure fiction, the money grubbers, who rule the world, want indebtedness not austerity.

Yet, austerity has become the accepted wisdom, a new panic to frighten the children. Across Europe nations receive accolades from the International Monetary Fund for tackling the excesses of the past and everyone looks the other way as the jobless eat from the garbage cans and the fascists rekindle the wisdom of another age.

Here in Britain, expectations have already been nicely adjusted, new food banks open daily and local authorities are to receive additional contingency funding to cope with the collateral damage during the adjustment phase as we all drift into dystopia.

And every night on our televisions we are told that there's no alternative to austerity. Frequently, the media gives air time to Mark Littlewood, the Director General of the Institute of Economic Affairs, a man who clearly would not register too highly on Dave's Happiness Index, a man certainly as mad as a box of spanners, possibly madder than Ayn Rand (she was the free market worm inside Alan Greenspan's head, as he watched the US banking sector go to the dogs and persuaded him to do nothing about it) and like Rand, Littlewood thinks that living at the margin for the majority is the only reality. Littlewood is the man from the school of rational expectations, i.e. expect little or nothing and you will not be disappointed.

Littlewood is also one of R D Laing's deluded individuals, seduced by the ideas of mad people but importantly, people like him are given the frequent opportunity to peddle the message that collateral damage is the price we must pay as we make the adjustment towards the new reality of Dave's brave new world, from rational expectations to limited expectations.

Footnote: Psychiatrist, R. D. Laing, once observed that the deluded man finds his delusions so obvious that he can't understand why the rest of the world doesn't want to share them. (*The Obvious*, Laing, 1968) Frequently, however, people do share the delusions of mad men, they believe things are as they are because it's obvious and then, they call it common sense - a shared understanding of the way they want the world to be.

Ending the Culture of Dependency

The Welfare Budget

The welfare bill is now nudging just over £200bn. (March 2013) Pensioners and children account for just over £100bn of spending but that they hardly fit into the scrounger profile.

The scroungers must be getting the other £100bn. Not quite, £18bn goes to support disabled people, through the Disability Living Allowance (DLA) and other benefits. This group are the genuinely disabled, not those receiving 'incapacity benefit', i.e. those parked by various governments, depending on the state of the nation. Add in money going to home carers, mothers on maternity leave, and help for the working poor and you have accounted for another £9b of non-scrounger spending. That leaves £53bn, from which we can deduct working tax credit, £8bn.

Jobseeker's allowance, income support and Employment Support Allowance (ESA is the new name for 'incapacity benefit') amounts to £21bn. Lastly, council tax benefit (£5bn) and housing benefit (£20bn).

Given that Atos Healthcare are being paid half a billion pounds to 'assess' those in receipt of ESA and DLA, the government clearly feels that this is where the scroungers are to be found.

The Welfare Reform Act (March. 2012)

The rationale for the Bill is simple: a large number of citizens have been on benefits for more than a decade, they have developed a dependency on benefits, they don't understand that work is good for them and need some encouragement to get back to work. So if they don't work we will take away their right to benefits.

"A life on benefits will no longer be an option for somebody. That system has got to change." Iain Duncan Smith (IDS)

A life on benefits has become part of our folklore and in order to buy in to the necessity of ConDem reforms, it's important that citizens support the idea of beating up workshy scroungers. However, it might be a good to also question the notion that a 'hard core' of long-term unemployed actually exists. Is IDS behaving like a conjuror, diverting public attention away from policy failure by blaming the poor for poverty.

It just might be that in order to dismantle the decades old consensus of the Welfare State, you begin by exaggerating the size of the bogey man, the long term claimant. However, the figures for people unemployed for five years have been falling for the past 10 years, in 2000 there were 48,000 long term unemployed claiming benefits, by 2010 that number had fallen to 4,300. (source ONS)

The size of the 'hard core' that concerns the ConDems so much is relatively small. So for now it might be a fair assumption that there's more going on here than meets the eye. Work and Pensions Secretary Iain Duncan Smith told us when he introduced the reform bill:"The publication of the Welfare Reform Bill will put work, rather than hand-outs, at the heart of the welfare system. Nobody will be worse off."

Very interesting, the Institute of Fiscal Studies said that 1.7 million people would be worse off?

Welfare Reform introduces some important changes, the notion of a Universal Credit is central. The idea will be to introduce a single payment that combines a number of existing benefits. Supposedly, a computer somewhere will work out what people are entitled to as their circumstances change. Progress on this scheme to date has been slow. Mr Duncan Smith excused the slow pace of introduction, saying that he had "reset" the scheme to ensure a successful roll out. The whole package contains many elements but at root it's designed to get the work-shy and sturdy beggars into work and JobCentre staff will be actively looking out for drug and drink dependent malingerers.

In some parts of the country, centres are being set up to provide 'food aid' for the poor. The food is provided by shoppers as they exit the supermarkets, how long will it be before the poor go shopping on their own account - chanting

Can't Pay? Wont Pay! This is now happening in Spain, thanks to the marvels of the Euro. In the interim period, until Job Centres are completely privatised, Job Centre staff have been told to make life very difficult for long-term claimants. In addition, long-term disability claimants are all to be assessed to gauge their suitability to work - this process is already underway.

Contracts have been handed out to 40 preferred bidders charged with finding work and training the long-term unemployed. The assumption here is that outfits like Serco, G4S and other service agents will be able to do a better job than the private agents formally charged with the job.

In terms of the Big Society, the idea is that Serco and Co. will parcel out contracts to voluntary and special agencies to deal with people that have learning difficulties and other handicaps that have prevented entry into the jobs market. The contracts rely on payments by results, which may cost between £3 and £5 billion pounds.

The case of A4e

A4e are one of the ConDem's chosen preferred suppliers for their Work Programme, through which A4e supposedly find work for people, and as long as those people stay in work for a few weeks, the company gets paid a tidy fee. Problem is, some A4e agents don't actually place people in jobs, they just say they have and claim their tidy fee, having filled out all the necessary paperwork themselves.

A4e's Work Programme contract with the government is worth millions and A4e is not the only company collecting money for finding people jobs, which quite frankly any halfwit could find by looking in a newsagents window. Point, these companies are not doing anything special and the money being wasted on their interventions would be better spent within the existing Job Centre system, specifically on staff training to focus their efforts away from processing people to actually finding people those elusive minimum wage jobs.

Bottom line, A4e have been fiddling the books, the fiddling is systemic across the country. The company lost its contract in May 2012 - red faces all round. However A4e only lost one contract, it still has contracts worth £500m - the Public Accounts Committee is investigating.

Give us the numbers (figures provided by DWP)

In Merton, south London, A4e found sustainable work for just eight people over nine months for which data is available.

Contractors like A4e are paid by results, so after a year in action, you might expect that the government would be keen to publish some performance figures - to demonstrate the success of the project. By the end 2012 only a partial picture of the success or otherwise of the programme has been provided.

Over the first full year more than 93,000 unemployed people went on to A4E's books. That alone netted the company more than £41m of taxpayers' money in "attachment fees". A4e found work for only 4% and were paid yet more money for this marvellous achievement. Note: "attachment fees" are paid for just having a name on the books, it does not mean finding them a job.

A4e are dealing with three groups: 18-24-year-olds claiming Jobseekers' Allowance, over-25s claiming the same benefit and the supposedly ill or disabled people getting Employment and Support Allowance who have been assessed as fit to work after all.

At the bare minimum they need to find long-term work for 5.5 per cent of all these kinds of claimants to hit the minimum standard set out by the DWP. This figure is the DWP's estimate of the numbers who would find work without any help. Company targets for 2013 and 2014 are 20% and 30% respectively. A4E have failed - they only found work for just over 3 per cent in 2012 for 18-24-year-old jobseekers, just under 4 per cent for the older group, and barely 1.5 per cent for the Employment and Support Allowance section.

In total, A4E has received £45,893,535 from DWP, most of that, as noted above, from the initial attachment fees. The cost to the taxpayer per job outcome so far is £13,498.

A4E aside, the picture for all companies involved in the Work Programme show that between June 2011 to July 2012, 878,000 people who joined the programme, only 31,000 found a job for six months or more.

Joining the work programme is mandatory for people aged over 25 when they have been out of work for a year and for under-25s after nine months. People in certain circumstances, like young offenders, must join after a shorter period of time.

Work for Free scheme is just wrong

The Back-To-Work scheme requires claimants on job seekers' allowance to take work with companies like supermarkets for no wages. Failing to cooperate leads to a loss of benefits. Well, university graduate Cait Reilly, challenged having to work for free at a local Poundland. Her case went all the way to the Supreme Court, where the government scheme was ruled invalid.

So the politicians passed some retrospective legislation to validate their scheme. In effect, the government criminalised the act of refusing to work for free. That's democracy in action!

Then in July 2014 the Court of Appeal said the retrospective legislation was unlawful and a breach of the Human Rights Act. The DWP were clearly not winning the argument but neither were they giving up and have no intention of repaying the £130 million of benefits they have withheld from job seekers.

What citizens need to understand is the fine distinction between a government infringing human rights and the public interest. The retrospective creation of criminal offences is prohibited under both international and domestic law but when the government appeals against the Court of Appeal decision it will justify it on public interest grounds.

Universal Jobmatch revolution

The government's Universal Jobmatch website was found to list duplicate and bogus jobs. A check carried out by Channel 4 News has found that a random sample of 2.7 million jobs placed on the site over 12 months, more than 650,000 offered duplicated descriptions.

Department for Work and Pensions (DWP) has acknowledge that more than 350,000 vacancies advertised breach its own conditions. Jobseekers' have to use the site if they expect to claim benefits. The DWP says of its website:

"Universal Jobmatch revolutionises the way jobseekers look for work. The vast majority of employers post genuine jobs, and we crack down on those who don't play by the rules."

Well actually, what it revolutionises is scrutiny since it enables JobCentre staff to track how often and how many jobs claimants are pursuing. Perhaps JobCentre time would be more profitably spent checking how genuine the job ad's on their site really are.

Jobseekers may find the website a trifle less than useless but hackers are finding it very useful, that is, for scramming the personal details of benefits claimants using the site. Data stolen via the site includes passwords, national insurance numbers and even scans of passports.

The contract (£15m) for running the Universal JobMatch website does not come to an end until 2015 and so the DWP has decided to do nothing, even though it is more than aware of how useless it is.

Vanishing jobs helpline

A helpline, set up to assist the unemployed to get back into work has been hit by the cuts but is not being upfront about its hours of business. Careers advisors working for Broadcasting Support Services (BSS), a private company running the helpline, were told to tell customers that there was no one currently available, when in fact there was no one there at all. BSS is funded via the government quango the Skills Funding Agency and Vince Cable has told them to investigate why they are not providing the service that they are being paid £9m a year to provide. However, it was the National Careers Service who left BSS short of staff, by making careers advisors redundant. We hope that's clear?

Government created the 'benefits culture'

Following advice from government officials, many were undoubtedly led to believe they were genuinely incapable of working.

In the 1980s and 1990s, the numbers of men claiming incapacity benefits rose sharply, increasing almost every single year, from 463,000 in 1981 to 1,276,000 in 1999. A significant proportion of these claims came from areas of the country which had seen the disappearance of productive industries, and the jobs that they provided. It's not feasible that so many people have actually fallen ill. Rather the welfare state was cynically soaking up these people, desperately attempting to offset their potential political anger at being unemployed by inviting them to view their predicament as a health-based problem instead. And of course, if you are claiming incapacity benefit (now called Employment and Support Allowance (ESA)) you wont show up in the unemployment statistics.

Work Capability Assessment

At the end of April, 2012, about 70,000 seriously ill, disabled people lost some or all of their £99-a-week ESA (Employment and Support Allowance) allowance. A new limit for receipt of the contributory allowance of 365 days was put in place.

The government aims to test all claimants' ability to work "some time in the future" using the controversial work capability assessments (WCA). If a disabled person is judged to be able to do some "work-related activity", then the household is means-tested for contributory benefits, i.e. to see if a partner is working more than 24 hours a week, which could lead to an end to benefits.

The WCA tests are designed to catch claimants out. For example, the question, do you brush your teeth regularly is used to assess manual dexterity. Questions about claimants TV viewing habits are used to attest to their ability to sit and concentrate for prolonged periods. Now even to the untutored mind that is a fatuous conclusion, seldom does any thing appear on television that requires an ounce of concentration.

By 2015 almost 300,000 people will lose out – saving the public purse almost £2bn a year. It will also mark the end of the idea that the welfare state is a piggy bank to be emptied in hard times. Citizens Advice chief executive Gillian Guy calls this a "betrayal" and argues for a rethink. According to the government's own estimates, 94% of people in the "work-related group" on contributory ESA will continue to need support for longer than 12 months. Even average earners will pay in more in taxes annually (£5,800) than they will be able to take out in ESA (£5,200) in the event of being disabled.... sorry, that last phrase should have read 'in the event of being "adjudged" disabled since having no arms and legs is no gauge of capability to work.

At least that's the view of Iain Duncan Smith, who announced May 2012, that he also intends to cut Disability Living Allowance and replace it with PIP, personal independence payments. DLA was intended to help people meet the extra costs of disability-related care and mobility but the system is being abused says IDS. Disability Rights UK says that at least 25,000 people could be forced to give up their work as a result of the drive to restrict payments, pushing up unemployment payments. Also, campaigners have raised concerns about the assessment process that IDS puts so much store in, where a blind person is called back frequently to see if their condition has improved.

The contract to carry out PIP assessment on behalf of the government is up for tender and worth between £300m - £1b over four years. Atos Healthcare is not doing too well with

ESA assessments (40% of cases going before a tribunal are overturned in the claimant's favour) will be at the head of the money grubbing queue.

Update, March 2013, on PIP contract: Atos Healthcare has got the contract and are now busy subcontracting NHS hospitals to carry out the work for them. You know it makes sense.

Note: DLA is far from generous. There are different rates awarded depending on the amount of help an individual requires. The absolute maximum benefit for someone with the highest level of both "care" and "mobility" needs would be £131.50 a week. To qualify, a person would need frequent help day and night, and be unable or virtually unable to walk. The minimum level of benefit is just over £20 a week.

The role of Atos

French company, Atos Healthcare has been contracted (£100m a year) by the government to assess ESA claimants' capability for work. Be aware, the good works of Atos are not exclusive to the Tory led coalition, the work actually began under New Labour in 2008. The difference is that under the Coalition it is now much harder to make a claim. Atos's work has come in for a good deal criticism. In 2011, a work and pension select committee described Atos as inspiring "fear and loathing" among claimants, and concluded that there had been "failings" in the service provided by the company, which had "often fallen short of what claimants can rightly expect". One MP on the committee described the process as "disastrous". Appeals against Atos decision can take a long time, between 2008 and

2011, 31 people died whilst waiting for a decision on their claims; these included cancer patients found fit for work.

An example of Atos's good work:

"One of my constituents suffers from Parkinson's disease. Anybody with even a very basic knowledge of this condition knows that it is incurable and progressive. It can be managed, but over time the sufferer's health will deteriorate. Things will not get better."

"My constituent has been assessed twice by Atos for his fitness to work. Both times he was found able to return to employment. Both times that decision was overturned on appeal. It is not difficult to imagine his anger at receiving a third letter shortly after his second appeal instructing him to present himself for a third work capability assessment. This time, he was assessed as being unfit for work. However, my constituent knows that he will likely have to go through the process again in a few months time." Reported in the Guardian by MP Tom Greatrex, Feb. 2012

Citizens Advice, who deal with the fall out of Atos decisions, are very concerned about the inaccuracy of Atos capacity reports. Particularly because these same reports are being used to assess claimants for other benefits, such as disability living allowance (DLA), which will be called personal independence payment (PIP) from next year. (Try to keep up) And going forward the main route for all disability benefits will be through ESA assessment.

(Source: *Right first time?* An indicative study of the accuracy of ESA work capability assessment reports, Citizens Advice Report, Jan 2012.)

Most recently, September 2012, a survey of 1000 GPs reported 6% of doctors have experienced a patient who has attempted - or committed - suicide as a result of "undergoing, or fear of undergoing" the Atos test, the survey also found 14% of patients had self-harmed as a result of the test. It's estimated that 2 million people are eligible for an Atos interrogation - so we can expect the number still alive at the end of the process to be much reduced. Factually, there is no end to the process because Atos will keep calling you back until you lose the will to live.

However, should you decide to appeal against an Atos decision, be heartened by the fact that the majority of appeals are successful and be heartily warmed to learn that the tribunal that hears your appeal will cost up to £14,000 per head. However, appeals can take up 6 to 9 months to be heard, and there is a high likelihood that as soon as you win your appeal you can expect to be contacted again by Atos, for another assessment - after all they haven't seen you for several months.

Atos and imaginary co-operation with disability groups

Claims surfaced that the private IT firm Atos made misleading statements about proposed co-operation with disability groups to help secure a £400m contract to perform disability assessments.

The Atos tendering documents reveal that the firm said it would work with a number of disability organisations to carry out eligibility tests for a new disability benefit but at least four of the agencies mentioned in the documents had no knowledge of or intention of working with Atos.

Disability Cornwall said:

"We would not consider working with an organisation which has caused so much distress to so many disabled people. We have also voiced our concerns about how Atos Healthcare were able to win contracts [and] implied it would work with organisations such as ourselves without first seeking permission from the organisations it quoted. We hope the pressure on the government to investigate the manner in which this tender was won is successful."

In its bid for contracts to provide assessments for PIP, which is due to replace the disability living allowance from 2013, Atos said it would be working in partnership with charities "such as" the Essex Coalition of Disabled People (ECDP), and the Greater Manchester Coalition for Disabled People (GMCDP).

A spokesperson for Atos Healthcare said:

"We would hope that disabled people and their organisations will work with us to make the delivery of PIP as smooth as possible for those going through the process. We are making contact with those named in our tender document to ask them to share their expertise and knowledge with us."

A spokesperson for the DWP said:

"The mention, or not, of any particular organisation in the bids to deliver PIP was not material in the evaluation. This had no impact on the result and there is no reason to review the competition."

So, the final piece of the plan to put an end to the culture of benefits is in place, now what we need is an economy that can supply the jobs for all the sick, lame and wounded being shed from the benefits system. Ex-claimants may find themselves in a very crowded market for disabled workers, given that the government also intends to empty out all the Remploy factories.

The new target for 2013: Tax Credits

At the beginning of 2013, Iain Duncan Smith, writing in The Telegraph told us:

"Labour's legacy on tax credits tells a sorry story of dependency, wasted taxpayers' money and fraud."

And why pray, did Labour behave so despicably?

"At the most basic level, Labour used spending on tax credits as an attempt to gain short-term popularity. It knew what it was doing – this was a calculated attempt to win votes."

New Labour says it was attempting to reduce child poverty but IDS supplies some evidence to support his claims, unfortunately they are way off:

"Tax credit payments rose by some 58 per cent ahead of the 2005 general election, and in the two years prior to the 2010 election, spending increased by about 20 per cent."

In the run up to the 2005 general election, based on official HMRC figures, tax credits increased of 8 per cent, not 58%. In the two years prior to the 2010 election, tax credits increased by 8.8 per cent, not 20%.

"Between 2003 and 2010, Labour spent a staggering £171 billion on tax credits, contributing to a 60 per cent rise in the welfare bill. Far too much of that money was wasted, with fraud and error under Labour costing over £10 billion."

Again, using HMRC figures, Duncan Smith is wrong again, the figure for the period was £147bn not £171bn. For some strange reason IDS included the Coalition's 2010-2011 spending on tax credits in his calculations.

However, if we put to one side the New Labour argument about the need to use these credits to end child poverty and replace the aim with a lame attempt to support a low wage economy with top ups, then we can see that IDS is on dangerous ground cutting benefits to low waged working families. Tax credits are a subsidy to employers, strip out all the props and you'll reveal the starkness of a failed economic system, failed, because it's dependent on state handouts.

The End of Atos

With appeals against Atos judgments standing at 600,000, costing the taxpayer some £6m, the company's decided to pull out of the its contract for making 'fitness-for-work' assessments. Maximus Health Services UK has been given a three-year £500m contract to carry on the good work of Atos. Maximus says it has inherited an 18 month backlog of claims. The company told the BBC that improvements would not happen over night: "It'll take some time to hire the healthcare professionals. The expectation is that in 12 to 18 months, we should be able to catch up on the waiting times…" Interesting that the DWP hands out a contract to a company that is not fully prepared to take on the job. We can only wonder if they will be re-employing the healthcare professionals shed by Atos? The Commons work and pensions select committee suggested in July 2014 that taking on a new provider would not solve the main problem with the ESA system, the assessment process is flawed.

The Underclass Crackdown

The underclass in Britain today have only one purpose, to provide the political class with an excuse to pursue their social engineering project, of which the benefit cuts form a substantial tool in reshaping behaviour.

The functionaries of New Labour's 'black hand' of political correctness and the puritan apparatchiks of the ConDem Party squirm like maggots in a fisherman's tin, when they have to acknowledge the salivating underclass scum smirking at them from rent free social housing squalor.

The underclass kill, drug, imprison and feed their own children to savage dogs or turn them into 20 a day nicotine addicts before they start school. They camp like Wilburys on the verge of an imaginary Internet world, creating ego-centric, self-regarding persona, waiting like parasites for the next helping hand to arrive - so they can eat it.

Marx described them as the lumpen proletariate, the depraved elements of all classes. Today's underclass are not elements dislodged from their social roots by economic upheaval, as Marx described. Today, the underclass are like tooth decay.
  They form a tribe like the armies of wandering vagabonds that Henry VIII killed with such glee. Latter day Marxists, with their syrupy liberalism believe the likes of Karen Matthews to be role models for independent living in the 21st Century.

Note: Matthews was released from prison in early 2012, after arranging the kidnapping of her daughter Shannon, in order to claim £50,000 in reward money.

Intervention is now the rationale for social workers

Today, social apologists of all descriptions seek to understand the killers of Baby P by appeal to the departmental handbook of individual needs failure. The handbook provides a tidy solution for the end of year review of the 'seen to be doing something' cycle. Successful reviews are based on the number of interventions by handbook operatives. The process of intervening becomes the rationale. During the intervention process no attempt is ever made to address individual needs failure, to do so would damage the self-worth of the case (underclass scum) and undermine an empathetic and healing discourse.

The history of the modern underclass, as a collection of failed individual misfits, is inextricably bound to Dave's social engineering project. We can say with some certainty that Henry VIII was no apologist and neither is Dave and his plans for the underclass are among his most strident.

The first rule of politics, create a panic before you do anything

Government officials said that the 'permanent and embittered underclass' might take their anger out on ethnic minorities. Then the government announced that it would train an army of therapists to deal with what it labelled 'the epidemic of anxiety' that the recession would cause. New Labour's Baroness Scotland warned that 'domestic violence will rise with increased financial worries'.

The Big Society requires more than anything else a positive mental attitude on the part of its citizens. The Underclass has an attitude problem, generational wallowing in a culture of benefits does not lend itself to an upbeat temperament. Current political rhetoric says, getting all these sturdy beggars back into work can only be good for them. It would also save a very big slice of welfare spending.

Cracking down on the Underclass - Phase one.

Chancellor George Osborne signalled a renewed crackdown on the "out of control" welfare budget. He plans to cut another £4 billion, after announcing an £11 billion cut in June 2010. His aim was to encourage people, who from some 'life-style' choice remained idle and living on State handouts, back into work. Osborne's master plan was to make £18 billion in welfare savings by 2014-15.

The main problem with this National Socialist strategy is that the work is just not there. However, there is also a key structural problem, long term scroungers are ill-prepared for the discipline of work and do not have the skills required in any work place. A further major problem will arise when those people who have genuine welfare needs get caught up in the cull of the underclass. Could be that George, the son of a baronet, is behaving like a mad knight errant, slashing left and right, ploughing his charger through sturdy beggars and deserving poor alike.

George says: "Of course, people who are disabled, people who are vulnerable, people who need protection will get our protection, and more." Nice sound bite but when George sends out his cuts diktat to his people on the ground he will have to rely on their ability to discriminate, to apply some intelligence and judgment to individual cases. Be in no doubt there will be collateral damage.

Taskforce to tackle Gang and Youth Violence

Theresa May, MP, Home Secretary and Minister for Women and Equalities finally launched (Nov 2011) 'Call Me Dave's' blueprint to intervene in the lives of tens of thousands of poor people. She published the details of how the Government intends to end gang and youth violence.

She has a crazy blueprint, she has a taskforce of a mere one hundred advisors and a miniscule budget. In total the budget for this scheme adds up to £11.2 million, that's £10 million siphoned away from other Home Office initiatives and £1.2 million of new money, to be used over 3 years to tackle gang crime against girls.

The brains behind this scheme is Iain Duncan Smith MP, Secretary of State for Work and Pensions. He says, "there is no quick fix" for the problem of Gang and Youth Violence.

You could download his report but I'll save you the trouble. Now, if you have a son or daughter involved in gang violence and they come to the notice of The Taskforce you can expect a knock on the door. Open the door and you'll find a Multi-Systemic Therapist (MSTs) waiting to swing into action.

We don't actually know what training these MSTs have had that enables them to save the family from what ails them but rest assured, they form part of a multi-agency intervention army. This emphasis on 'multi-agency' is vital because it enables the lead agency, i.e. the Home Office to spread the load in terms of finance and responsibility. Hidden within the report is an unspoken assumption that up to 30 agencies, who at some time or another, come into contact with young people who might, potentially, become drug dealing knife wielding raping nasty bastards by the time they reach 15 years old will receive intervention along the way. In short, their sickness will be spotted and dealt with - an end to Gang and Youth Violence.

A return to a by-gone age of roaming vagabonds: The Second Phase

Millions of welfare claimants are set to have their benefits scrapped and replaced with a single "universal credit".

Under the changes, housing benefit, income support, incapacity benefit and dozens of other payments will be swept away in a major reform programme intended to break the culture of welfare dependency by making work pay. The intention to reduce housing benefit will have a major impact on the life of the underclass, forcing many to move out of the centre of towns to the margins, i.e. no doubt based on the Paris District 13 model. A key advocate of benefit cuts is historian David Starkey.

Starkey has said (filmed for BBC's This Week) he believes "the poor" should live in areas where they can find work. He wants "the poor", the man servants and the kitchen maids to move out of the gentrified Islington squares to roam around the nation seeking out job opportunities.

And, fundamentally, he insists "the poor" must ditch their values of fairness and entitlement - it's all gone far enough, too far! They, "the poor" expect to remain idle, living in properties (among their betters) that they will never be able to afford without state support - they must roam. Starkey is a 'better' and he knows best what's good for "the poor".

Starkey is on message, asking his audience to revalue the meaning of words. New Labour began the process of newspeak. Telling citizens which words could no longer be used, telling citizens how to think about things correctly. What Starkey is doing is adding intellectual support to the ConDem cuts agenda. Telling citizens, forget what you were entitled to and what you thought was fair, adjust to the new reality.

Clearly Starkey is advocating a return to the days of his hero, Henry VIII, and a return to the days of armies of wandering vagabonds. And everyone, except historians like Starkey, knows how Henry dealt with the embarrassment of these 16th Century job seekers. They were hacked down in the fields by his knights.

This is not the 16th Century, it's all far too complex for the superficial analysis provided by Starkey. The poor of Islington are being contained by welfare handouts, these local handouts prevent the disturbance that would be caused by wandering and roaming. That's what the welfare system is in place for, to consolidate the indigent poor, to keep them holed up watching their flat-screen tele's 24/7 and not out roaming around upsetting the Somali tourists, that one sees so many of in Islington.

Perhaps Starkey would like to see a District 13 on the outskirts of London, like the one seen in the futuristic French film in which the underclass are marginalised within a walled ghetto - the film was described by the Daily Mail as "socially clueless drivel" - that translates into "a bloody good film".

It would appear that Starkey was hooked by the drivel of Grant Shapps, one time Tory Social Cleansing commissar, his cleansing programme is now well underway. A report from the BBC suggested that most inner London boroughs are moving hundreds of people out to the capital's margins, or further afield to Wales. Kennsington and Chelsea have already dislodged 800 souls, some of them lifetime residents in the area.

Send For Pickles: Phase three of the crackdown

Communities Secretary Eric Pickles is to spearhead a ferocious crackdown on 120,000 problem families who blame everyone but themselves for their miserable behaviour. Pickles obviously will not be doing any work himself, he has a new quango for that, the Troubled Families Team.

Just how Pickles came up with the figure of 120,000 is just a mystery. Does anyone believe that he has an address book with a 120,000 names in it, probably not. Pickles is using the cover story that these 120,000 troubled families are costing us all £9 billion pounds a year. Another mystery, how the figure of £9bn was computed.

What he actually intends to do is off-load the identification of these families to England's 152 Local Authorities, who he intends to pay a finder's fee, plus a bonus for fixing the problems like, anti-social behaviour, school truancy, life-long benefit scrounging, etc. And he's got a big pot of money to dish out, around half a billion pounds. The councils have been instructed to draw up their intervention plans.

Pickles says: 'Sometimes we've run away from categorising, stigmatising, laying blame. By what criteria does our Eric plan to categorise, stigmatise, and lay blame?

They are low income, no one in work, parents with no qualifications, mother with mental health problems, one parent with long-standing illness or disability and if the family can't afford basic food and clothes. So we are going to categories, stigmatise, and lay blame on people for being poor or ill?

These indicators of "multiple disadvantage" were drawn from research by Tony Blair's Social Exclusion Unit and take note, no connection was made with anti-social behaviour, crime or truancy, etc, that was made by the current Department of Education to support Tory anti-poor prejudice.

The Daily Mail tells us:

"The councils will get £3,900 if they can achieve at least 85 per cent school attendance for children from problem families, a 60 per cent cut in anti-social behaviour and if youth offending falls by a third. Getting one adult from the family off benefits and into work for three months would earn the council £4,000."

Now, no one expects the Mail to spot that there's nothing in what it says that meets the actual criteria used to identify these families in the original research, from eight years earlier.

Making progress on Troubled Families

Dave's crackdown on the most troubled of families is turning into a most marvellous success, well, at least according to everyone involved in the scheme. As of April 2014, big Nick Pickles and his team had managed to identify up to 109,000 troubled families and we are told that 29,000 were no longer 'troubled'.

The government said its efforts were "on track" and having a "big impact" but the Public Accounts Committee said it needed to speed up. The thing is, Dave said that 120,000 families would be turned around by 2015 and with only eight months to go things are not looking that clever. For one thing they still have to identify 9,000 and then turn around 81,000; whatever turn around means.

Louise Casey, Head of the Troubled Families Programme had this to say:

"This programme is getting to grips with families who for too long have been allowed to be caught up in a cycle of despair. These results show that a tough, intensive but supportive approach has a big impact; giving hope and opportunity to the families and respite to the communities around them."

Good use of language there from Louise and one supposes that you need to be tough when you are saving people from a cycle of despair. And be in no doubt Louise is tough, showing no mercy to family members who attempt to resist.

We need to remind ourselves at this stage that this scheme is costing half a billion pounds, with local authorities and others being paid on a payments by results basis. Again we may wonder, by what criteria will success be signed off and paid for. Who for instance will do the checking, surely not the same people being paid to deliver the results - don't bet against it. We do know that local authorities have struggled to find families who match the criteria set by the scheme and so have been allowed to add some local criteria to meet their quotas. And we need to remind ourselves that Pickles was saying that the figures provided by local authorities are not 'official' - that's worrying.

The only certainty in all of this is that 'troubled families' make good headlines for the right-wing gutter press. The latest count tells us that the Wilburys now number half a million and cost us £30bn a year. Louise Casey believes passionately that her interventions can make these people good and useful citizens, even if they do not want to take part in the big society. It could be that these families are not troubled in the least but rather it's Louise Casey that's troubled.

These people did not just fall to earth in last winter's rains, they are products of this society. Dave's Troubled Families Team is a disgraceful reminder of the way we do business and perhaps, it's the way we do business that needs intervention.

The 2013 Cuts

Bedroom Tax

Anyone on housing benefit, with a spare bedroom, is faced with a choice, move or start paying for that empty room, alternatively they may choose to become a foster carer or sub-let the room and become a landlord. Housing benefit was cut by 14% for one extra bedroom and 25% for two or more extra bedrooms.

Council Tax

Also, and this may come as a shock for those intent on becoming a landlords, support that they may have been receiving for their Council Tax is being reduced by 10%. Staggeringly, nearly 6 million households are claiming this benefit.

The Social Fund

Parts of the Social Fund will be abolished, including Community Care Grants and Crisis Loans. Local authorities will be given money to spend on local schemes such as food banks and to provide subsidised furniture and white goods.

Benefits cap

Increases in all benefits will be capped at 1%. So with inflation averaging 2.7% (RPI), if you believe the government, start spreading the marg' a bit thinner. And a little known fact here, most of those affected will be people in work, because it includes tax credits.

The Institute for Fiscal Studies tells us, 2.5 million households without someone in work will lose an average of £215 per year in 2015-16, while seven million households with someone in work will lose an average of £165 per year.

Total Benefits Cap

As from the 15th April, 2013 four London Boroughs will pilot the new annual £26,000 total limit on benefits and out of work family can claim. Duncan Smith says this is only fair as scroungers shouldn't be earning more in benefits than the average of those who actually get up in the morning. However, he's not being honest, because working families are receiving tax credits and this takes the average wage to £31,000 not £26,000. However, going forward the plan is to reduce the cap to £23,000.

Universal Benefit

This will replace the following benefits: Child Tax Credit, Working Tax Credit, Housing Benefit, Income Support, income-related Employment and Support Allowance, income-based Jobseekers Allowance and parts of the Social Fund.

This benefit will paid monthly and will be constantly under review by a new computer system, that currently is not working properly, so that as claimants circumstances change, so will their benefits. The people of Tameside, Oldham, Wigan and Warrington will be the guinea pigs for this one.

No new claims for Tax Credits will be accepted after April 2014. Claims will have to be made for Universal Credit instead

From mid-2014, it was hoped that all new benefit claims across the country would be for Universal Credit? Sadly, for Iain Duncan Smith that moment never came to pass; his plans for UC are in disarray and he's in denial.

Disability: the torment continues

Those who support the cuts will be heartened to learn that the torment dished out to disability claimants by Atos Healthcare will continue apace. Atos have just received a new contract to administer assessments for Employment Support Allowances and they have been good enough to sub-contract this work to various NHS Trusts.

The Disability Living Allowance (DLA) is being replaced by the Personal Independence Plan (PIP) and some 30,000 disabled citizens will have their benefits reduced as a result. PIP will be introduced in Cheshire, Cumbria, Merseyside, North East England and North West England for people who are very ill or disabled and who need help with day-to-day living. It will gradually replace Disability Living Allowance

(DLA), which is currently paid to under-65s who have daily care needs or difficulty getting about. Not everyone who gets DLA were not able to get PIP and after June 2013 no new DLA claims were being taken.

And here's a nice twist, anyone still in receipt of DLA in October 2015 will have to apply for a PIP, if its refused, their benefit will cease.

Benefit Cuts and income elasticity

Dave's apprentice chancellor, George Osborne, is unable to make any distinction between skivers and strivers. Osborne's cuts in benefit will hurt more people in work than at home in bed. Cameron, Osborne and Duncan Smith persist with their claim that everyone on benefits is part of what they brand as the "dependency culture".

Boy George fails to grasp the basics of economics, people working for minimum wages spend proportionately more on items such as food, heating, transport and rents than those who shop at Harrods, all these items are necessities and the overall impact of George's benefit cuts will be dire. Dire because the incomes of the poorest will be driven down, making work a more pointless enterprise for these people and instead of reducing the numbers of skivers, who keep George awake at night, he'll see a big increase to haunt his dreams and spending in the high street will take a dive.

Unintended consequences

Manipulating the public's outlook has been quite successful, up to a point. However, some of Dave's policies have not yielded the desired results and in some cases have turned out to be perverse. He was hopeful that few beyond the hacks at the Guardian and the Independent have noticed.

Labour had not noticed the many complications arising from Dave's policies since all they cared to complain about was the 'cost of living crisis'. And as long as Labour insist on allowing Ed Balls to keep uttering his refrain about the economy flatlining, instead of putting forward, at least one radical alternative to the same old tosh, the result at the next election is in the bag for Dave.

At this point we need to remind ourselves that Labour are full square behind Dave in his efforts to give benefit claimants a good thrashing. For instance, Labour believes that Universal Benefit is a marvellous idea. However, private landlords are not so sure because under this scheme the rent goes to the claimant, not the landlord. This idea is causing not a few landlords to become a bit jittery, well, the drug addicts, alcoholics and scallywags can't be relied upon to pay their rent in preference to enjoying themselves - just one more time.

However, Dave has a plan to help out private landlords, introducing new legislation to make evictions easier. This is probably not his soundest scheme, when we consider that the court system is already being overrun due to lack of resources and perhaps more importantly, there are now more private tenants than social housing tenants. Why, because the social housing stock has dwindled to such an extent that councils are being forced to rely on private landlords to house the homeless.

Bless those landlords, they really are being besieged on all sides, the benefits cap is also causing them to rethink their letting policy. Claimants having their benefits capped increases the likelihood that they will default on the rent - might be better to evict them and let to foreign workers - key word, workers.

Currently, January 2014, Universal Benefit is still at the pilot stage, having suffered from some kind of computer malfunction. When UB goes nationwide, the combined impact of that and, the benefits cap, on the private rented housing market could be significant, as thousands of people are turfed out by their landlords. No doubt local authorities are already gearing up for this eventuality?

Bedroom tax

Local authorities, bless them too, are already busy dealing with the fallout from another of Dave's policies gone wrong, the 'spare room subsidy', otherwise known as the bedroom tax.

Imagine a situation where a couple have a one room ground floor flat with a garden and they want to transfer to a two bedroom. Many have declared an interest to downsize due to pressure from the spare room subsidy but were unable to exchange with the one bedroom couple because they were in rent arrears and you can't swop homes if you are in arrears but they were put in arrears by the government's policy.

However, government policy on social housing is fatally flawed by the fact that the number of smaller properties that people are expected to move to just do not exist. A number of housing associations in parts of the long gone industrial north have larger properties sitting idle, leaking revenue for months on end, soon they'll be calling in the bulldozers - the cheapest option.

Loophole, do you mean black hole?

In the meantime, IDS wants the names of whoever it was that missed the loophole that allows anyone who has lived in a property for 17 years to ignore the bedroom tax. More than a slight error since up to 40,000 could be exempt from the tax. Be assured, the loophole will be closed forthwith or as quickly as it's possible to get a piece of legislation through parliament - let's call it two years then.

Objective criticism

In September 2013, the special UN *rapporteur* was very critical of the bedroom tax. Raquel Rolnik, the UN inspector, says she has never faced such an aggressive, hostile reaction from a government before. She was here to investigate social housing provision. Rolnik observed that the bedroom tax was causing great hardship and distress to the most vulnerable. The Bavarian Wing of the Tory party called her names. They just couldn't appreciate someone from Brazil casting a spotlight on their shadowy misdeeds. However, people's lives are being seriously disrupted and damaged by this coalition's penny pinching bedroom tax. The discretionary payments, that are supposedly in place to protect those in real need, i.e. the disabled and chronically sick, are insufficient to meet all the claims. At least one third of those claiming a discretionary payment are being refused.

More UN criticism (August 2014)

The UN Committee on the Rights of Persons with Disabilities launched a formal probe into whether this country has committed **'grave or systemic violations'** of the rights of disabled people. Tory MPs said Britain's record on help for disabled people was among the best in the world. They claim this is proven by spending amounting to £50bn a year on the disabled. They did not tell us how many billions they are paying out to their private sector sub-contractors.

The Future of Welfare

What sort of world do you want to live in?

As from April 1st, 2013, people reliant on benefits will take a pay cut. According to Iain Duncan Smith, it's for their own good, hand outs are no good for anyone, what people need is a hand up. For Duncan Smith, a world without benefits is fairer for everyone - we hope that's clear.

Beyond the 19th century paternalism of Duncan Smith, as necessary to his existence as CO_2, we hear George Osborne telling us that we simply can't afford the £200bn plus welfare bill. Totally unaffordable!

Well, how much would be affordable, how much of the welfare spending is vital and necessary; and importantly, how much of the welfare bill is actually a subsidy to employers paid to their employees to keep wages down.

Time to stop and think

The world that Beveridge was looking at was vastly different to that of today, the material conditions of life were more basic, as were the expectations of the working class - back then, still able to identify itself as such. You were in work or you were out of work. In work you had some meagre assurance that you had food on the table and a roof over your head, out of work was nowhere, out of work you were a stranger in your own land. Beverage's world was not utopia but it was a big improvement over what preceded it.

It's interesting to note that Tory hero, Benjamin Disraeli, wrote in his 1845 novel, *Sybil*: "the only duty of power, the social welfare of the PEOPLE."

It took several decades, however, for the wealthy and privileged to realise their responsibility towards the less fortunate in society. Although, society didn't exist and that's what Disraeli was writing about, the need for something more than the uncaring indifference of those in power and their wealthy backers.

By slow degrees those who ruled recognised the need to provide support for those who needed help, beyond the whims, wonders, and sanctions of charitable giving. In Whig terms, the welfare reforms of the Liberal Party between 1909-1914 were ambitious; an old age pension, unemployment and sick pay, based on national insurance contributions. It wasn't much, some crumbs from the table that was paid for. And it's worth remembering the Work Houses were still there but their name was changed to Poor Law Institutes, for those who fell through the cracks. And we can also find traces of Iain Duncan Smith's ideas in the shape of the "Seeking Work Test", introduced in 1921, full unemployment benefit was only paid upon evidence the recipient was looking for work.

The workers mainly took care of themselves, through the a vast network of Friendly Societies and trades unions. The Church of England also played a major role in alleviating poverty and distress. The Poor Law system began to fade away by 1930 but was not formally abolished until 1948. That was when something approaching social democracy finally began to emerge in Britain. Meaning, that for the first time in British history, government took responsibility for the welfare of its citizens and was prepared to redistribute the national wealth in pursuit of the goals set out by the Beveridge Report: to end Want, Disease, Ignorance, Squalor and Idleness. Let's consider that a work in progress.

And the point is?

The post-war government at least had a plan and set out in detail what they were trying to achieve through their reforms. The current government has no plan except making cuts to benefits and making life difficult for millions of citizens, in particular, those caught up in the 'bedroom tax' nonsense and genuinely disabled people.

The supposed savings from benefit cuts will be eaten away by payments to the private contractors, employed to police the new system, the likes of A4e, G4S, Atos, Serco etc, and for computer systems that don't work. Tribunal appeals against Atos for its woeful Work Capability Assessments has already cost millions of pounds. With the change from DLA to PIP we can expect the costs to increase all the more with the likes of Capita and Atos in the driving seat.

Talk of benefit cheats and scroungers, is just verbiage inserted by Tory spokesman and fellow travellers, in place of a meaningful rationale for the cuts. Benefit cheats are few, certainly not significant enough to transfix the whole Tory party, while they ignore the £70bn and more lost through tax evasion/avoidance.

Affordability

The persistent argument that the welfare bill is unaffordable displays an understanding of economics that falls short of a C grade. Not that we have ever been told how much would be affordable. What we have been told is that some benefit is unaffordable, the bit that goes to the undeserving and no one has told us how many Wilburys we are here talking about.

The £200bn of spending on benefits is unaffordable if you view it as a handout, money given away, never to be seen again. This is the logic of the current government, how often have we heard the refrain "a hand up, not a hand out" that's what people need. Fine, but benefits are not a 'hand out', they are largely transfer payments in recognition of the fact that income inequality in Britain shames everyone. And what do the benefit recipients do with their windfalls, they spend them in the shops here, they don't put it in offshore tax havens. On second thoughts, benefits payments may end up offshore, if they are spent in Top Shop.

Conclusion

Cutting the welfare budget will do nothing to correct Britain's national debt and that debt is the key issue for Dave. The coalition's fixation with the structural deficit is another piece of obfuscation, the national debt is rising because we are not selling enough to pay our way in the world. We borrowed on a promise and got caught out, the whole ship of state was suckered by the snake oil peddlers, well it happened and it needs to be dealt with and picking on some poor people will not fix Dave's 'broken Britain'.

Is a world without benefits possible? There are those down at the Institute of Economic Affairs who believe that such a world is possible. We do not know if the current government wants to end all but an 18th century regime of outdoor relief.

We do know that they say the current benefits bill is unaffordable. Yet, they are unable to tell us what is affordable? This may actually mean that they do not know what they are trying to achieve through their current hostility towards benefits claimants.

The Tory Record to Date

Economic Policy

Tory economics is a credo that places blind faith in the power of the market place and seeks reassurance from charlatans and errant number crunchers who have a worse track record than Mystic Meg. The phrase 'Open for Business' best sums up the irresponsibility of Tory economics, allowing foreign owners to snap up key assets and then repatriate their revenue to some low tax hide-away.

'The plan is working'

The plan is working means that there are signs that the economy is beginning to grow again although the ground lost since 2008 is a long way from being regained. However, no degree in economics is required (as George has proved) to engender some growth in Britain plc. The City of London is the counting house of the world, the City of London is Britain's Treasure Island. Forget Paris, Bonn, Hong Kong etc., the City has an independence that other financial centres envy. The growth of new technology start-ups in mobile apps and games is also making a significant contribution to Britain's rise from the ashes.

Add in the magnetic attraction of London and the South-east generally for the world's wealthy elites, as well as, advantageous tax incentives prevailing for foreign business as they queue to sell their products into Euroland. Add in the low-wage costs, zero hours flexibility and wage subsidies, then small wonder that we have signs of growth. Part of the plan was to spread growth more broadly across the nation, away from the reliance on the South-east corner - this is not happening and there's nothing in place to make it happen. The idea that building a high-speed train line to some mythical 'power house' in the North is part of the solution to 'rebalancing' is just fatuous.

The truth is that Dave does not have a plan for the economy. Tory economics is based on free market star dust, hope, osmosis and the Chinese. Mark Carney and his tea and biscuits committee have done nothing for five years, except print money. Carney's negative real interest rates have damned savers, distorted exchange rates and provided the money grubbers with cheap money to create a housing bubble.

Tax Dodgers

Talk of benefit cheats and scroungers, is just verbiage inserted by Tory spokesman and fellow travellers, in place of a meaningful rationale for the cuts. Benefit cheats are few, certainly not significant enough to transfix the whole Tory party, while they ignore the £70bn and more lost through tax evasion/avoidance. We hear tough talk at party conferences about dealing with the dodgers, so far there's been no action.

Justice system

Just the facts: Prisons

England's 124 prisons are holding 86,000 souls. That population has doubled in the last twenty years. England locks up far more people than any other comparable European country. Over half of all prisons are overcrowded although prison minister Jeremy Wright tells us "we have enough space within our prisons to accommodate all offenders". Yes, minister, and there's enough space on the Isle of Wight to accommodate half the world's population, as long as no one wants to sit down. Staff shortages are a major problem, both in terms of maintaining control, the health of staff and even pretending to run a rehabilitation programme. The ratio of prison officers to prisoners in 2000 was 1:2.9, by the end of September 2013 this had increased to 1:4.8.

Staff shortages are compounded by the mental health of many inmates, 90% of whom are said to have some type of mental ailment; which is made worse in turn by the free availability of drugs of all descriptions. Rehabilitation is not working, 49% of all those leaving prison reoffend within one year.

You may recall that Dave told us: "Prisons will become places of hard work and industry, instead of enforced idleness." Well, enforced idleness is the norm, fewer than 10,000 inmates are gainfully employed within the prison estate.

And for our corporate friends

The Legal Aid Act sets out Dave's plan to look after his corporate friends by making it harder, no impossible, for poor people to take on big companies, including media corporations through the courts. For instance, parents of babies brain-damaged at birth due to dodgy medication or victims of human rights abuses at the hands of Britain's security services will not be able to pursue the guilty. Dave is selling this legislation as an attack on ambulance chasing lawyers, as seen on afternoon television, as an attempt to reduce motor insurance premiums. The coalition's cuts to the legal aid budget are not just unfair, they are undemocratic, denying access to the justice to a whole swathe of poor citizens.

Policing

Mr Cameron addressed a Police Federation gathering thus:

"Britain has the bravest and best force anywhere in the world."

Would that be the same police force that some quarters are telling us we need a Royal Commission to investigate. Investigate things like "the fabrication and destruction of evidence, deaths in police custody, framing of suspects, abuse of databases for personal reasons, punitive attitudes to innocent members of the public, abuse of the Taser stun gun, contempt for legitimate protest, examples of racism and use of excessive force and restraint ..." (Henry Porter, The Observer, Sunday 20 October 2013)

Home Secretary Therasa May told the Police Federation that the government would cease giving the Federation £180,000 a year, having discovered that it had several millions sloshing around in its bank accounts. We can only wonder why government would be giving gift aid to the enemy within.

Bottom line: the police service across the whole country is not performing well and Mr Cameron is ignoring its failure.

Transport policy

A vibrant economy needs to move people and goods around the nation efficiently. Britain does not have a vibrant economy, neither does it have a transport policy. What Britain has is projects and cones. It has a quango, the Highways Agency, responsible for moving the cones around. It has a Department for Transport, responsible for projects. It doesn't have a transport policy.

High Speed 2: Unquantifiable strategic benefits

Dave sent former Transport Secretary, Philip Hammond, to Birmingham to launch what he called "one of the most extensive consultations in history" it was a strange day because the decision to build the £xxbn (insert your own costs) High Speed 2 rail link, between Birmingham and London and beyond to Leeds. The day provided us with a new piece of political speak from Hammond, "Unquantifiable strategic benefits", that he said is what we should expect from HS2. If the benefits are unquantifiable might it not be better to get someone to figure out the benefits before spending unknown billions on the idea?

Justine Greening moved into Hammond's chair at transport in October 2011, she was as unqualified to be in charge of transport as he was.

"Our vision is for a transport system that is an engine for economic growth, but one that is also greener and safer and improves quality of life in our communities."

She had a vision, not unexpectedly it involved privatising the road network. She said it was all about "the feasibility of new ownership and financing models for the strategic road network." and naturally, she found time to utter the usual Tory claptrap: "this will lead to increased investment and driving further efficiencies in the network." Justine was no doubt a visionary but she was also a third runway blocker, so she had to go.

No sooner had Patrick McLoughlin taken possession of the national train set from Justine, the wheels came off and this time we couldn't blame Railtrack and Jarvis. No, this time it was those silly mandarins at the Department of Transport, apparently they made a mess of the franchising process for the West Coast Line. And the cost of their little mistake to the tax payer? Estimates range between £40m and £100m.

Energy

Hope and osmosis will not do it, we need energy!

The British economy has a number of problems that are not being addressed, many due to the political mistakes of the past. In particular, the privatisation frenzy of the past 30 years that saw the sell off of natural monopolies like energy to an oligopolistic cartel has been a disaster. Dave's best option of the moment was to ditch his pledge to become the 'greenest government ever' and remove 'green taxes' from consumers' energy bills. This tactic was forced on Dave by Ed Miliband's pledge to freeze energy prices for two years and to reshape the energy market, if Labour were to be elected in 2015.

But being Dave he counter-balanced his negative reactive position with some positive citizens' advice. He told poor people, who can't afford their energy bills, to put an extra jumper on. He also suggested that they might like to try one of those price comparison websites that he has heard tell of. And getting really technical, he suggested people might like to fiddle with their thermostats. Saving the best until last, he announced his 'huddle and heat' scheme, whereby citizens only heat one room and huddle together for warmth. Dave seemed to be unaware that stark temperature differences between rooms causes condensation, this in turn leads to mildew. Dave is also unaware that mildew is a parasitic fungus that will cause illness in the very young and old. He also does not know that price comparison websites do not necessarily provide the best deals, they provide the deals that pay them a commission on sales.

Current energy policy, such as it is, is easy to sum up: half-hearted renewables, heavily subsidised nuclear rebuilding, coal, fracking and imported gas. Don't expect the lights to stay on 24/7 past 2025.

Britain's energy policy is in the grip of the Gaia panic, the imagined imperative that the planet must be saved from man-made pollution. This panic has given rise to a form of tokenism to appease the planet god by building wind turbines at fantastic expense, in the certain knowledge that they will never produce enough electricity to boil a kettle of water, a tokenism that sets fanciful targets for reducing emissions so far into the future without a hope of achieving the goal.

Climate change

So good has the global warming marketing campaign been that only a mad person will dare to question its truth. Saving the planet is the new religion, the scientists its apostles, the politicians their acolytes. The people will cooperate without any opt-outs, the need for action on climate change outweighs individual preferences, indeed individual preferences will be shaped to favour pro-planet activity, e.g. driving your car five miles less a week, fitting dull light bulbs etc. Saving the planet is the only rational consumer choice.

James Lovelock, the man who developed Gaia Theory disagrees with the consensus view. Lovelock says the planet is a self-regulating organism, that has managed fine without help from climate controllers for millions of years and it does not need any help now. If he's right, there's an awful lot of people wasting their time and being paid good money for nothing. And all the Eurocrats who sanctioned trading in carbon credits should be arrested.

Pointing to the flooding of the Somerset Levels as evidence of climate change is nonsense. If the flooding was evidence of anything it was the management failings of the Environment Agency and Tory cost cutting.

Immigration

As a member of the EU we have little choice over our degree of welcome, we could become a tad less tolerant as a policy measure and then all learn to speak French. There in lies Dave's problem, tolerance lays at the heart of British culture (it might just be apathy or indifference?) so we need to retain our attitude towards foreigners.

Dave promised to reduce immigration to tens of thousands by the end of this parliament, he will almost certainly fail. Ms May's silly 'Go Home' vans really did not help the problem. Most recently he says he will put an "emergency brake" on EU immigration, he's got more chance of winning the lottery.

NHS

The Tory pledge for the NHS was that spending would be protected, not cut. Since the creation of the NHS, spending has increased on average by 4% a year. Over the this parliament, the increase will be 0.1%, so not a cut!

The Act has opened the flood gates for the private sector to take increasing share of the health care market, feasting like parasites on the infrastructure and administration developed over past decades. Mr Cameron talks with passion about protecting the NHS, whilst allowing the private sector to masquerade behind signs saying NHS Hospital. The claim that the NHS is not being privatised by stealth is pure nonsense, the advent of the Any Qualified Provider scheme testifies to this. So far over one hundred private companies have been given the green light to ply their services under this scheme.

Child protection

This is one of the biggest areas of policy failure of this and every other government down the years. The only time politicians talk about these failures is when high profile cases like Rotherham or old friends of Cyril Smith then every thing goes quiet again. Children in care are not being cared for and the political class are ignoring it.

Old people

What to do about old people is another major area of policy failure, specifically the design of a care package for the last years of citizens lives. The mistreatment of elderly citizens in hospitals and private care homes is also a cause for national concern but just as with children in care, the situation mainly gets ignored. One quarter of care homes are providing inadequate care, the residents of these waiting rooms for death would be better off camped in a local park, perhaps then someone might take their plight seriously.

Pensions

New Labour wrecked the private sector pensions market with Gordon Brown's raid. The death of defined benefit schemes came in an instant, in a foolhardy act of vandalism. Gordon Brown's abolition of tax relief on pension funds' investment dividends was far more criminal than the earlier Tory mis-selling, his action managed to destroy one of Britain's few success stories. As a direct consequence of Brown's action, employers started closing defined benefit (DB) schemes, offering defined contribution schemes in their place, and then closing DB schemes to existing members - leaving millions of pensioners poorer in their last years as returns on shares and gilts felt the impact, annuity rates fell. This one act destroyed the pensions industry. The banker's recklessness led to cost cutting behaviour by businesses and forced increasing numbers to switch from defined benefits to defined contributions schemes.

It's worth noting that the earlier Tory regime's privatisation mania also made a mess of the pensions industry. And the current Tory contribution has been to attack public sector pensions, with everyone working longer for less. And the impact of George Osborne's recent changes to the requirement for people to buy an annuity is far from certain.

Defence

Among all government departments the Ministry of Defence must be first in the queue when it comes to a cost cutting cull. It's failure to control inventory was highlighted more than 20 years ago and despite spending £1.1bn on a new computer system for stock control, the situation is no better today. According to a PA committee in 2013, the ministry had over £6bn of stock that it doesn't need. This ministry has made an art form of out of making a mess of procurement and wasting billions of tax payers money. It is also making mess of recruiting a part-time army to replace all the troops being made redundant under the current regime.

Foreign policy

Britain does not have a foreign policy. Currently, the Foreign Secretary writes letters to despots and tyrants telling them that their behaviour is unacceptable, sometimes he does not write letters to nasty people for fear of causing upset, it just depends whether they have nuclear weapons or not. It also depends on whether they buy lots of nasty weapons from us like Saudi Arabia. Some cynics might suggest that we just go along with every foreign adventure that the US decides is of geopolitical importance. We may also add to these strands the tactic of total silence when it involves our own misdeeds, e.g. the Chagos Islands or deals done and Royal Pardons given to IRA killers and definitely, no mention will made of the mess we leave behind after our good work is done, e.g. Iraq, Libya, and Afghanistan. And we really do not want to talk about the effectiveness of sending a few planes to assist with the bombing of ISIS, IS or ISIL in a circumstance where the troops on the ground are inadequate to the task of defeating the Jehadi caliphate.

Sport and the Olympic Legacy

Basking in the glow of Team GB's Olympic success Dave came over all passionate about the need to encourage the young to participate in sport and become the next generation of Olympians.

Sounds good but we do know that the coalition has phased out the School Sports Partnership scheme, saying that it wasn't delivering, they have also ended free swimming for under 16s. We do know that they are cutting £1bn of funding to councils for spending on sports and recreation. And we also know that Call Me Dave has discontinued the New Labour target of two hours of PE for all children, on the grounds that the target was being met by items like 'Indian Dance', not proper competitive sport.

We also know that they are committed to encouraging inter-school competitive sports. The primary school curriculum is being revised to make inter-school competition mandatory.

The School Sports Survey suggests that Dave may have a point. However, Dave has now abolished the School Sports Survey, making it difficult to know about school sports participation in the future?

4G Roll Out

Back in 2010, then culture secretary, Jeremy Hunt told us that the UK would have "the best superfast broadband network in Europe by 2015". This left people who know about such things wondering what he meant by the word best. Subsequently, Hunt revised his language and replaced best with fastest. One of Hunt's Baldricks must have told him that the word best covers a host of variables (price, coverage, speed and market choice), meaning it might be difficult to achieve. Hence, his choice of fastest may be considered a smart down grade to his ambitions.

Currently, Britain has an average broadband speed of 24Mbps, about the same as Bulgaria and a lot less than many EU countries. For Mr Hunt's information, superfast means 100Mbps and not just in the cities. That could take some time to achieve, perhaps ten years.

Unfinished Business

Chilcot

The Iraq Inquiry, also referred to as the Chilcot Inquiry after its chairman, Sir John Chilcot, was a public inquiry into the Britain's role in the Iraq War. The inquiry started in November 2009 and came to an end in February 2011. We are still waiting for Chilcot's report to be published. Big Dave wants to catch sight of the Chilcot Report by Christmas 2014, as does everyone else. Well, that is, not the Labour Party since it will not do much for their election chances and definitely not Tony Blair, who really does not want to be visited by the ghosts of Christmas past. However, it may be worth recalling that Dave and his Tories all backed the invasion of Iraq. Note: Christmas came and went and still no sign of Chilcot's report.

Leveson: and the point was?

The Leveson Inquiry was initiated following the convictions of News of the World royal editor Clive Goodman and private investigator Glenn Mulcaire for the illegal interception of phone messages. Evidence began to emerge that the activities of Goodman and Mulcaire was common practice within the newspaper business. The hacking of Milly Dowler's voice mail was the last straw and so the Inquiry began in July 2011.

Leveson concluded that the Press Complaints Commission was not up to the job of press regulation and suggested a new independent body, of which membership would be voluntary.

We do not know the true cost of the Leveson Inquiry, the official government figure is £5.4 million, this has been under estimated by a few millions. The first part of Leveson's report was published in November 2012. Since then the press cohorts have not been queuing to sign up to the new scheme of things. All very confusing, do we have a replacement for the PCC or not, if so, what is it?

Deficit reduction

You may recall that the coalition was going to disappear the budget deficit by the end of this parliament. They reviewed the situation two years in and decided to postpone the demise of the deficit to 2017/18. This was a good move since the nation is currently spending more than it is receiving and this situation is unlikely to change for some time. The problem in a nut shell is that the tax-take is not growing with the growth of the economy. Low pay zero hours flexibility may be good for business but it's no good for the exchequer. Can I hear you thinking, well surely the tax-take from all the firms benefiting from a buoyant economy must be making a larger contribution to the tax coffers - well, no, revenue may be up by 200% but taxable profit is the same as it ever was - all very curious?

Bottom line

The coalition have made the eradication of debt the rationale for its austerity programme. The structural deficit is not being reduced, the national debt is increasing, further austerity for you is assured.

Reflections on Dave's Plans

This is Dave's Britain in 2014

Dave's project to dismantle the state and farm out its functions to private contractors continues apace, the long term effects for Britain will be a disaster. The changes that Dave has introduced to date should not be underestimated. When the earlier Tory government privatised all the utilities and the rail network, the changes were immediate and appeared obvious. This time round the changes are more subtle and far from obvious and far more wide ranging, affecting the whole social fabric. How aware are the voters of 2015 of these changes, affecting the health service, the justice system, the police service, child protection, defence, border control, the benefits system and soon, work and pensions. This is the state divesting itself of all direct responsibility for the day to day management of civil society; is this what "decentralising control" means?

We need to remind ourselves how all this is justified in the Tory mind:

"We will base our plans on the same insights that are driving reform across Government: increasing competition; decentralising control; enhancing transparency; strengthening accountability; and paying by results."

The use of the word reform adds the suggestion that the changes being made will improve the existing state of affairs. However, the idea that increasing competition will be the catalyst that drives efficiency and productivity forward is patent nonsense. Competition is a part of a zero sum game, it has no place in health and social care, unless you view human beings as commodities to be traded by 'any qualified provider'. Over a hundred firms have been given AQP status in the NHS. This we are told will increase patient choice. For that to happen the patient needs perfect knowledge, already we see some services being offered by multiple agents in a single area, in these circumstances even doctors will struggle to choose a provider. The most likely outcome of Tory health reform will be the fragmentation of the NHS and then it will not be a national health service any more.

Public Health minister, Jane Ellison, told us in June 2014:

"I don't know how much any of you realise that with the Lansley act we pretty much gave away control of the NHS, which means that the thing that most people talk about in terms of health [the NHS] ... we have some important strategic mechanisms but we don't really have day-to-day control. One thing is clear, no one voted for a Coalition government and no one voted for the wholesale reform of the NHS either."

The Baldricks behind the Tory reforms have the audacity to use the word 'insights' to describe the underpinnings of their zealotry and that's all it is, zealots genuflecting to the money grubbers. The private companies now running much of the public sector are not transparent, not accountable and they will take their penny whether they achieve the results set for them or not because they operate beyond oversight - but this is Dave's world and you're in it.

Note: for some facts on the far reaching extent of outsourcing, see *The Shadow State* by Zoe Williams, 2013., available on the web.

Dave's reign is like an absurdist play, akin to *Waiting For Godot*, waiting for Dave to fix broken Britain, whilst dealing with 'moral collapse', using nothing more than black swan thinking, horizon scanners, patronising behavioural psychologists, nudgers, snoopers, endless panics and celebrities wandering into the austere wasteland with their messages of hope - Dave's like Wilkins Micawber, waiting for something to turn up.

What nearly turned up was the end of the United Kingdom, due to Scotland's independence referendum in September 2014, which was only narrowly won by the No vote. The Scots' may have said No to independence by a small margin, perversely, they said a much bigger No to Westminster politics. The disinterested and arrogant behaviour of the three main party leaders may have played a part here. The historians will tell us for certain but it looks likely that Dave has made a mess of things Scottish.

Now all he has to look forward to is the 2015 General Election, well that and his very own referendum 2017, when British citizens will vote to leave the disastrous European Union – assuming that Dave keeps his Referendum promise? It is more likely that he will claim to have renegotiated away all our problems, far too complicated to explain to the citizenry, so no referendum required. All of which assumes that Dave wins a second term and that the SNP let him have a referendum?

The End

For now, form a queue and hope that when you get to the front, to acquire the latest transformational App, it might just change your life but don't hold your breath - well, not for more than four minutes.

The political process under Dave continues to be a pointless charade, devoid of vision, big ideas and utopias and, definitely no new Camelots. Dave's Big Society has now gone to landfill.

All you can expect the next time you vote is more of the same; further shrinkage of the state, further outsourcing of responsibility to private corporations, and further erosion of social value as profits are siphoned off to foreign shores. Be in no doubt, all of the blunders of the past; Thatcher's disastrous Poll Tax, the franchising of the rail network, Blair's PFI hire purchase schemes, Brown's destruction of the pensions industry are as nothing to Dave's cunning plans.

If you are young, why should you worry, there's no hope for you anyway, you're being cast adrift by the ship of state, you're just unaffordable. New Labour turned your local bus shelter into a university and some fool of a Tory said they could charge you up to £9000 to take shelter and you did, then they sold your loan to a bunch of private equity cowboys. Now your options abound, spend the next 30 years in a low paid job, they'll write off your debt, move around a lot, that will confuse them, or take out a direct debit and wonder every time they take piece of your wages why you thought that attending a bus shelter was a good idea.

If you are young, pay attention, pay attention to the maltreatment of the elderly; don't imagine that your future will be more sublime. All the future holds for you is a rendezvous with reality, with built in zero hours, low wage flexibility and definitely no gold plated pension.

Pay attention and above all, beware the obvious lest you start calling it common sense and a politician sneaks up on you and pokes you in the eye. And before you can say ouch, I will say, serves you right … if it was that obvious, why didn't you see it coming?